The Peak Dist
Youth Hosteller's Wal

by

Martyn Hanks

The village of Foolow

Martyn Hanks is a professional model-maker living near Preston. His work has taken him from London to Australia, Saudi Arabia and the Caribbean. A strong desire to travel has led him to visit over 100 countries, youth hostelling in many of them.

Martyn is a member of the YHA Northern Region Council. These walking maps resulted from a wish "to give something back" to the YHA. Encouraged by YHA staff, he has now mapped most of the youth hostels in the north of England. His other two Youth Hosteller's Walking Guides, *The Lake District* and *Yorkshire Dales & Moors,* are currently published by Landmark.

Martyn has also held several exhibitions of his paintings including exhibits at the Harris Art Gallery, Preston and at the University of Central Lancashire.

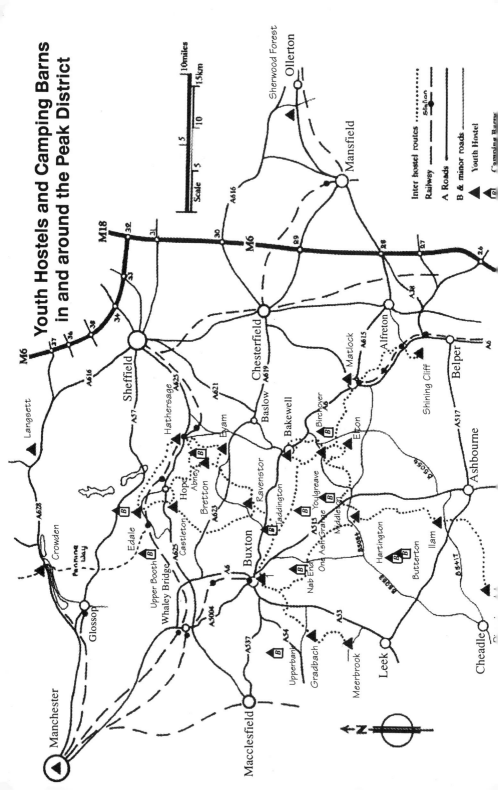

Youth Hostels and Camping Barns in and around the Peak District

The Peak District Youth Hosteller's Walking Guide

by

Martyn Hanks

Castleton Youth Hostel

Published by:
Landmark Publishing Ltd,
Waterloo House, 12 Compton, Ashbourne,
Derbyshire DE6 1DA, England

ISBN 1 901522 35 0

British Library Cataloguing in Publication Data:
A catalogue record for this book is available from the British Library

Printed by J. W. Arrowsmith Ltd
Designed by James Allsopp

Acknowledgements

The publishers wish to thank the following for their assistance: Colin Logan, YHA Chief Executive; Liz Lloyd, YHA Business Development Director; Gill Chapman and Barbara Southam at YHA Northern Regional Office.
The walks have been sourced from out of copyright maps supplied by Michael Bell of Bells Bookshop, Halifax, Yorks (01422 365468).

Safety Note:

The majority of the walks in this book are low level. It is strongly recommended that the OS map be carried on all high level walks which should be avoided in bad weather.

Title Page Illustration: Castleton Hall Youth Hostel

Situated in the heart of the village, it offers traditional dormitory accommodation plus upmarket ensuite family rooms in the adjacent old vicarage. The latter is available for hire out of season.

Key to maps

- ▦ —Wooded area 🌳
- G-Gate ▨▨▨
- S.-Stile ▨▨▨ ▨▨
- SP–Sign post ⌐
- ╪—Bridge ◠◠
-)⸝— View point
- Ⓣ Telephone ☎

Foreward by Colin Logan, Chief Executive of the Youth Hostel Association of England and Wales

I am sure that many readers of this invaluable and interesting guide book will need no reminding of the importance of Youth Hostels to our National Parks and other wonderful stretches of countryside. Indeed many of you will be taking advantage of the YHA's network of accommodation in the Peak District as you read it.

Others of you may feel that you are too mature or too fond of your creature comforts to darken the doors of a Youth Hostel. Or perhaps you have only partly happy memories of school trips of many years ago and a recollection of a spartan regime in which it was mainly the shared discomfort which engendered camaraderie!

The YHA continues to serve the needs of hundreds of thousands of walkers, cyclists, schoolchildren, families, foreign backpackers and myriad other travellers every year. The accommodation remains simple and affordable by all but it is also comfortable, welcoming and well maintained. In an area such as the Peak District we offer a unique and incomparable range of experiences in terms of the location and setting of our properties.

As our President, David Bellamy, wrote recently "While others have recently discovered the concept of sustainable tourism, our aim from the start has been to instill knowledge and love for the countryside, and an understanding of the deeper values associated with our environment and heritage".

Much of the time you may be more concerned with the tiredness in your legs or the shortness of your breath. But when you pause to take in the fantastic landscape views which the walks described in this book offer you, I am sure that you will think of these deeper values — as indeed you will when you arrive at a Youth Hostel after your strenuous day out and enjoy the warmth of hospitality and companionship to be found there.

I hope that you enjoy this guide and find the walks from it to be rewarding.

CDC Logan

Contents

Walks around Youth Hostels

Inter-Hostel Walking Routes

"What is the YHA?"

"To help all, especially young people of limited means, to a greater love and care of the countryside, particularly by providing hostels or other simple accommodation for them in their travels, and thus to promote their health, rest and education". These aims, set out when the Youth Hostels Association first began in 1930, remain as important as ever. The Association grew from the dedicated effort of visionary people and provided a firm foundation for recent years which has seen great strides in upgrading and the development of new hostels.

Images are often outdated — of spartan surroundings, rules and regulations and a belief that hostels are only for young people. Today, a Youth Hostel signifies good value accommodation which is friendly, comfortable, dependable and secure, backed up by an assurance of standards which apply to Youth Hostels around the world.

The 237 Youth Hostels throughout England and Wales provide a major national resource. Together, they account for over 14,000 bedspaces which places the YHA in the top league of accommodation providers. But it is the location of the hostels which makes them a truly unique asset. Over the years, sites have been found in some of our most spectacular landscapes, in remote hill country, on Heritage coasts, or lowland woodland settings. Many Youth Hostels are in villages or small towns, where they are close to the countryside but also are accessible to other facilities and form part of the local community. The hostels in the Peak District range in size and comfort from 17th-century manor houses in the prettiest villages to a former mill in an unspoilt and little-visited corner of the wilder areas of Derbyshire: many are in incomparable locations ideal for walkers.

As a body of some 270,000 members in England and Wales, the YHA is a social movement, enabling people of all ages to meet others in a special atmosphere of friendship. The international movement, of which YHA England and Wales forms a part, is rightly seen as a force for peace and understanding. Membership of YHA England and Wales entitles people to travel and hostel in over 60 countries around the world with more than 5,000 Youth Hostels to choose from.

While others have recently discovered the concept of "sustainable tourism", the aim of the YHA from the start has been to instill a knowledge and love of the countryside and an understanding of the deeper values associated with our environment and heritage. This has always come first; our accommodation is a means to an end. Increasingly, there is a wide range of types of hostel, clearly indicated so that members can select which one is likely to meet their particular needs. Yet throughout, our firm principle is that the simple, recognisable character of Youth Hostels is always retained.

From its inception, the YHA has been an environmental movement which has worked with its own resources to implement sustainable tourism principles in practice. We have a seven point Environment Charter for Youth Hostels worldwide which underlines our commitment to important issues such as reducing consumption, recycling and conserving energy.

The Youth Hostels in the Peak District exemplify the YHA with their wide range of opportunities to explore all parts, from the bustling market towns of Bakewell and Matlock to the remote and little-visited moors.

The YHA is a member organisation and you will be asked to show your membership card on arrival at a Youth Hostel. If you are not already a member, you can join at the first Youth Hostel you visit or alternatively contact YHA for a membership form (you will find a special voucher entitling you to a free one year's membership on the last page of the **Lake District** book in this Youth Hosteller's Walking guide series). You will receive a free annual guide listing all the hostels in England and Wales and receive a regular members' magazine and discounts on travel, places of interest and shops.

Booking your stay is easy — simply telephone or write to the hostel of your choice. Alternatively, from most hostels you can book a bed ahead.

When you stay at a Youth Hostel you will sleep in comfortable bunk-bedded rooms sharing with people of the same sex, unless you have made special arrangements in advance — for instance, families or groups of friends may be able to acquire rooms with fewer beds, often with their own washing facilities. Otherwise, you will find showers, toilets and washing facilities close to your room. You will be given freshly laundered bed linen with which to make up your bed. Pillows, duvets and/or blankets are also provided.

At most Youth Hostels you will find comfortable sitting areas for relaxing and socialising, as well as facilities such as drying rooms, cycle stores and local information. While many hostels have areas specially set aside for smoking, there are also many "No Smoking" hostels. At small Youth Hostels — to keep prices low — you may be asked to help with simple household tasks. You are asked to clear up after yourself.

Circular routes from hostels are popular with walkers who like to spend several nights in one place, exploring the countryside from their base. If you are a member of a walking club or simply a group of friends and family, you can choose in the winter to rent a whole Youth Hostel for your group under the YHA's 'Rent a Hostel' scheme. Some of the smaller Youth Hostels in the Peak District are available — with a key for you to come and go as you please and good self-catering facilities for all your meals. A brochure on 'Rent a Hostel' explains how to book and is available by 'phoning 01727 855215.

YHA has spent considerable sums of money refurbishing its buildings and improving standards of comfort and privacy. Each year, more hostels are identified for improvement, a few more properties open for business for the first time, and those surplus to requirements are closed.

Today YHA is a vibrant organisation catering for the needs of young and old. So long as you are young at heart, a warm welcome awaits you!

Liz Lloyd
Business Development Director

Haddon Hall

WALKS AROUND HOSTELS AND INTERHOSTEL ROUTES

Walks around Castleton   (OS Outdoor Leisure Map 1)

Castleton to Hope and Lose Hill   6.5 miles (10.5km)
Map 1 (see pages 14 / 15)

At the end of Hope Valley, the path turns to climb out of the valley and to the top of Lose Hill. It then proceeds towards Mam Tor before descending back to Castleton.

Take the path described in the **walk to Hathersage YH** down the side of the Peakshole Water to Hope village — your only refreshment stop on this walk. Take the Edale road past the school before turning left to start the walk to Lose hill. Beyond the railway to the cement works, it starts to climb, becoming much steeper beyond Lose Hill Farm.

The path goes straight to the top where you can marvel at one of the best viewpoints in the Peak. The whole of the Hope and Edale valleys lie below you, Kinder Scout stretches away to the north and the Eastern Moors can be seen beyond the Derwent Valley. If you are wondering where are the other good viewpoints, look no further than Win Hill which guards the east side of the entrance to the Vale of Edale. It is slightly lower than Lose Hill.

From here the path follows the ridge via Back Tor to Hollins Cross. Continue on to Mam Tor, if you wish, and look out for the surrounding ditch which defended an Iron Age Fort there. From Hollins Cross the path descends straight down to Castleton. It is an old packhorse route dating from around 1455 which is known as Hollowford Road.

Castleton to the Show Caves
Map 2 (see pages 16 / 17)   5 miles (8km)

This short walk goes up Cave Dale from the Market Square. At the top, it turns left to follow a wall to the A625. The path continues on to Windy Knoll before turning right and recrossing the A625. Mam Tor towers above on your left as you descend to the Blue John Mine. Mam Tor is called the Shivering Mountain because of landslips; you can see how the old turnpike road slipped once too often and had to be abandoned.

The path continues around Treak Cliff to the Treak Cliff Cavern, which still mines Blue John Stone and has a cave system discovered during mining operations. Continue on to Speedwell Cavern, an 18th-century lead mine entered by boat. From this busy cavern, the path returns to Castleton past the entrance to Peak Cavern, a huge natural cave system.

Castleton, Edale & Mam Tor
Map 3 (see pages 18 / 19)   7 miles (11km)

A good walk, not long in distance but with memorable views and lots to look at en-route. The path climbs up the old packhorse route to Edale (See next walk for further details). From Hollins Cross you can detour left to Mam Tor — the defensive ditch of its Iron Age Fort may be seen. Drop down into Edale, where there is a good information centre.

Climb back up to Mam Nick, west of Mam Tor, and descend to the A625 to join the path back to Castleton via the show caves (see previous walk). From Treak Cliff Cavern, it is worth a detour to where the old road has been abandoned. An interpretation board explains why. Look for the

10

crushing circle to the former Oden Mine to the right of the road (marked by a circle on the map). The mine should not be entered it is very old and dangerous. Note the alternative path back to Castleton from the crushing circle.

Castleton YH to Edale YH

Map 4 (see pages 20 / 21)   5 miles (5.75km)

A short and direct route to Hollins Cross on the Mam Tor to Lose Hill ridge. The path then descends into the Vale of Edale directly to Edale YH, with an alternative diversion to Edale village.

    The route out of the village and up to the ridge between the Hope and Edale Valleys is an old packhorse route dating from aroun 1455. Mill hands working at the Edale Mill also used it to walk to work. Prior to the construction of Edale Church, coffins were also brought by packhorse from the Edale area to Castleton Church for burial. The passage of many horses has eroded the path into a holloway, hence its name, Hollowford Road.

    Walk through the churchyard and turn left. Cross the A625 and take the road ahead. It is heading for the dip or gap in the high ridge in front of you, known as Hollin's Cross. There is a well defined track all the way up the hillside. The Cross marked the junction of several packhorse routes but it has gone. From here the path descends to the right via Backtor Farm to the valley road. Turn right, go under the railway bridge and continue down the road to the hostel drive on your left.

    Alternatively, from Hollins Cross, a path bears to the left as it descends into the valley. It heads directly to Edale past Hollins Farm. There is a National Park Visitor Centre in the village plus two pubs for refreshments. Paths run from the Nag's Head pub and the Information Centre to Ollerbrook Booth Farm where they join and continue on directly to Nether Booth and the youth hostel.

Castleton YH to Hathersage YH

Maps 5 / 6 (see pages 22 / 25)   8.5 miles (13.5km)

This path goes down the Hope Valley before going south to Bradwell and then over Abney Moor before dropping down to Hathersage. There are impressive views from the moor towards Kinder Scout and the Eastern Moors.

    Leave the village on the A625 before taking a path to the right to follow the Peakshole Water. Upon reaching Hope, the route diverts briefly onto lanes before following the river again, higher up the hillside. Just before crossing the final field to reach Brough, the path crosses the site of Anavio, a Roman fort. There is not much remaining although Peveril Castle in Castleton contains some bricks thought to have been taken from here.

    From Brough, take the path into Bradwell, the last stop for refreshments. Turn left just beyond the church and climb up onto Bradwell Edge — a fairly steep climb, but the views make it worthwhile. The path joins Shatton Lane for a while, then turns right to cross Abney Moor before turning north to Offerton Hall and the descent to the River Derwent just outside Hathersage.

    Cross the fields below Offerton Hall to reach the stepping stones across the river to the A625 a short distance from the youth hostel. If you know that the river is likely to be high, take the detour from Offerton Hall shown on the map, or simply follow the river downstream from the stepping stones to reach Leadmill Bridge and the road into Hathersage.

Castleton Y H to Bretton YH & Eyam YH   (OS Outdoor Leisure Map 1 / 24)

Map 7 / 8 (see pages 26 / 29)   Bretton 7 miles (11km)   Eyam 8.5 miles (13.5km)

Take the path to Brough described in the **Castleton YH to Hathersage YH walk.** Cross the B6049 Brough to Bradwell road and take the path to Bradwell church. From here it climbs up onto Abney Moor, passing Robin Hood's Cross. The path joins an old track called Duper Lane which leads to Abney, where one leaves the path which leads on to Hathersage YH.

From Abney, a small hamlet, descend Abney Clough to Stoke Ford. Climb out of the valley up Bretton Clough to reach Bretton YH and The Barrell Inn (if required). The map shows the route following the road for much of the way to Eyam from Bretton. However, the alternative route shown on the map is on an unmaintained road over Sir William Hill and offers a quiet and safer option.

Castleton YH to Ravenstor YH   (OS Outdoor Leisure Maps 1 & 24)

Maps 9 / 10 (see pages 30 / 33)   9 miles (14.5km)

This walk takes you over the high ground between Castleton and Peak Forest. It then follows a long dale with a succession of names which runs down to Miller's Dale.

Leave Castleton up the dry Cave Dale below Peak Castle, heading for the open fields at the top end of the dale. The path soon starts down to Peak Forest through an area of old lead mines. Keep clear of these as you walk down the green lane to the village. Note the alternative route shown on the plan. This involves some walking on the busy A623 which is not recommended.

From Peak Forest, cross the fields opposite the pub heading for the top end of Dam Dale. After joining a track for a short distance, it changes its name to Hay Dale and then Peter Dale.

Crossing the Tideswell to Tunstead road, the dale becomes more wooded and deeper and is known as Monk's Dale. This section is a nature reserve and includes some rather wet areas (off the path) which support a different habitat*. A section of Monk's Dale crosses an area of boulders and rocks. It is reasonably easy walking so long as you watch where you place your feet. Eventually the path reaches Miller's Dale village. Cross the B3049 road to Tideswell and walk down the side of the River Wye before turning up into the hostel drive.

*They occur where, unlike limestone, the underlying rock is volcanic and impervious to water penetration.

Walks around Edale   (OS Outdoor Leisure Map 1)

Edale, Mam Tor & Hollins Cross   6 miles (9.5km)
Map 11 (see pagess 34 / 35)

A walk up the valley to Edale village and then a climb to Mam Tor for magnificent views of the Hope Valley and the Vale of Edale.

The hostel is situated about a mile from the village at Nether Booth. The booths were outlying farmsteads of which there are several in the valley. Walk to the village through the fields. It is fairly flat, so make the most of it! The village Information Centre is worth visiting before heading up Harden Clough for Mam Tor. There is an Iron Age encampment on the top and the large ditch around it can still be seen.

From Mam Tor, walk along the ridge to Hollins Cross before descending down to Backtor Farm and the valley road.

Alternatively, the walk may be extended by continuing along the ridge. This walk is described in the text to Map 20.

Hollins Cross, Lose Hill & Edale End

6.5 miles (10.5km)

Map 12 (see pages 36 / 37)

This path takes in Lose Hill to the south-west of the youth hostel and then descends into the Vale of Edale at Edale End. A detour can be made to Hope village for refreshments.

Climb up to Hollins Cross from the hostel and turn left on the ridge-walk to Lose Hill. This is an ancient packhorse route from Chapel-en-le-Frith and Hayfield to Hope and then on to the east. It cuts below the top of Lose Hill from Back Tor. The recommended path goes to the top of Lose Hill, one of the highest vantage points south of Kinder Scout with memorable views in all directions.

From here either descend to Townhead and turn left to reach the road near Bagshaw Bridge at Edale End, where the National Trust has an interpretation centre and its local estate office. From here it is a little under two miles back to the youth hostel. As an alternative, note the path heading from Lose Hill to Hope where there is a pub, cafe and toilets. You can also catch the train here to return to Edale, if you prefer.

If not, once suitably refreshed, take the Edale road before turning left to join the path to Edale End mentioned above.

Map 13 Hathersage Village Plan (see pages 38 / 39)

Walks around Hathersage

(OS Outdoor Leisure Map 1)

Hathersage to Stanage Edge

9 miles (1 5kms)

Map 14 (see pages 40 / 41)

This walk has the option of a reduced 7 miles (11kms) length and a return journey by train from Upper Padley. The route goes up onto Stanage Edge and enjoys memorable views before descending to Padley Gorge.

Walk up the main street, bearing left at the Nat West Bank to reach Baulk Lane. Follow this out of the village past Brookfield Manor and then North Lees, a four-storey tower house typical of several built in the Peak. Buxton Hall, adjacent to the Crescent in Buxton, is another example.

Climb up onto Stanage Edge and follow the well trod path along to Higger Tor and then Carls Walk, with its Iron Age encampment and large defensive wall. Look for abandoned millstones and even troughs — they litter the area around here.

Upon reaching the A625 you can divert to the left for a short distance to the Fox House Inn or continue on to the lovely Padley Gorge. The path is very popular as it descends down through the wood. At the bottom, there is a cafe near to the railway station.

If you are continuing on by foot rather than by train, look out for Padley Chapel — all that remains of the forteenth- century Padley Hall. The path continues up the river meadows close to the River Derwent to return to Hathersage. This is a rewarding walk, especially on a clear day.

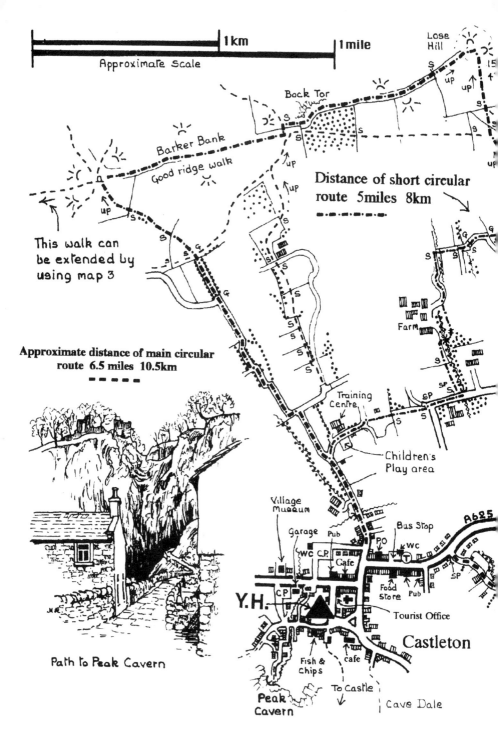

1 km   1 mile

Approximate Scale

Lose Hill

Back Tor

Barker Bank

Good ridge walk

Distance of short circular route 5 miles 8km

This walk can be extended by using map 3

Approximate distance of main circular route 6.5 miles 10.5km

Farm

Training Centre

Children's Play area

Village Museum

Garage   Pub   Bus Stop

WC   C.P.   PO   WC

Cafe   T

Food Store   Pub

Path to Peak Cavern

Y.H.   C.P.

Tourist Office

Castleton

Fish & Chips   cafe

To Castle

Peak Cavern

Cave Dale

A625

14

Map 1
Castleton to Hope and Lose Hill
see page 10

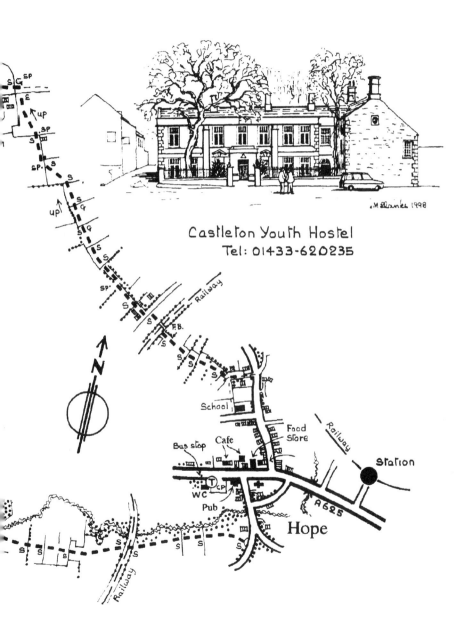

Castleton Youth Hostel
Tel: 01433-620235

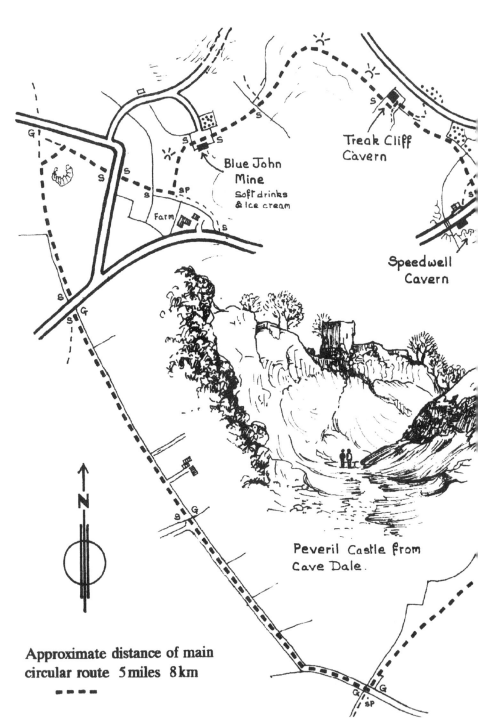

Treak Cliff Cavern

Blue John Mine

Soft drinks & Ice cream

Speedwell Cavern

Farm

N

Peveril Castle from Cave Dale.

Approximate distance of main circular route 5 miles 8 km

- - - -

Map 2
Castleton to the Show Caves
see page 10

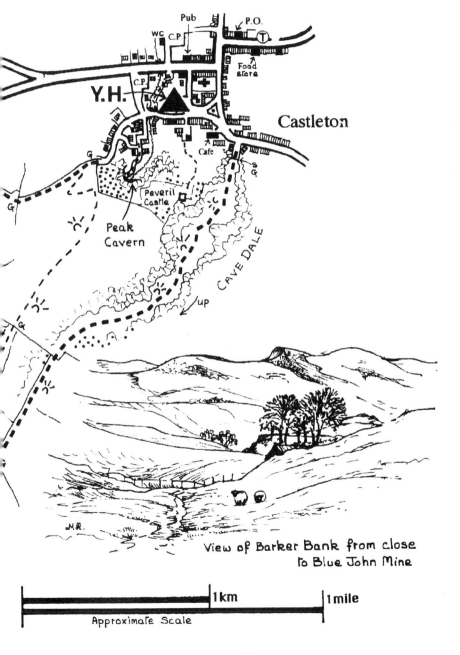

View of Barker Bank from close
to Blue John Mine

Peak
Cavern

Peveril
Castle

CAVE DALE

Castleton

Y.H.

Pub

P.O.

WC

C.P.

C.P.

Food
store

Cafe

up

1km | 1mile

Approximate Scale

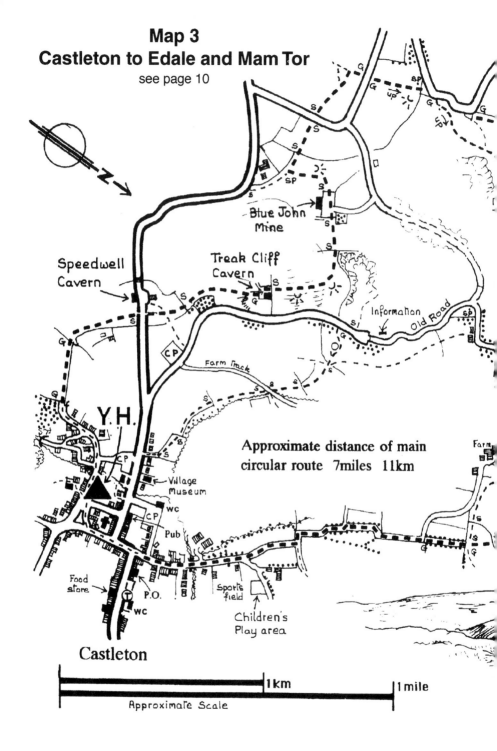

Map 3
Castleton to Edale and Mam Tor
see page 10

Blue John Mine

Speedwell Cavern

Treak Cliff Cavern

Information

Old Road

Farm Track

C P

Y.H.

Approximate distance of main circular route 7miles 11km

Farm

Village Museum

wc

C P

Pub

Food store

P.O.

wc

Sport's field

Children's Play area

Castleton

| 1km | 1 mile |

Approximate Scale

18

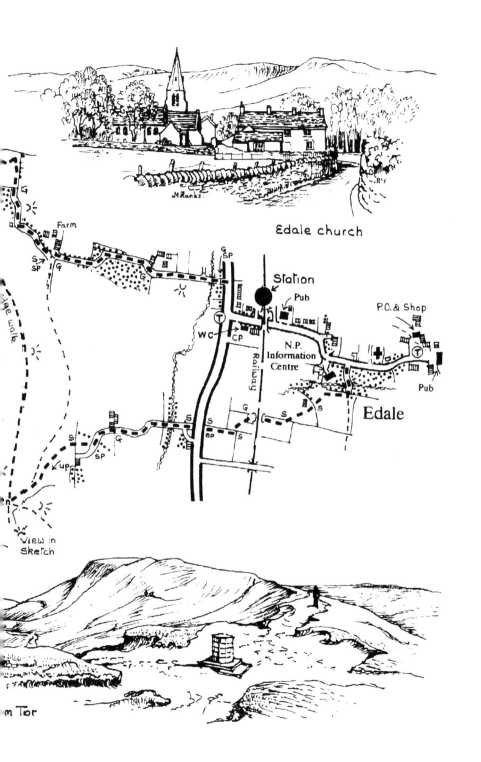

Edale church

View in Sketch

Farm

Station

Pub

P.O. & Shop

N.P. Information Centre

WC

CP

Railway

Pub

Edale

m Tor

Map 4
Castleton YH to Edale YH
see page 11

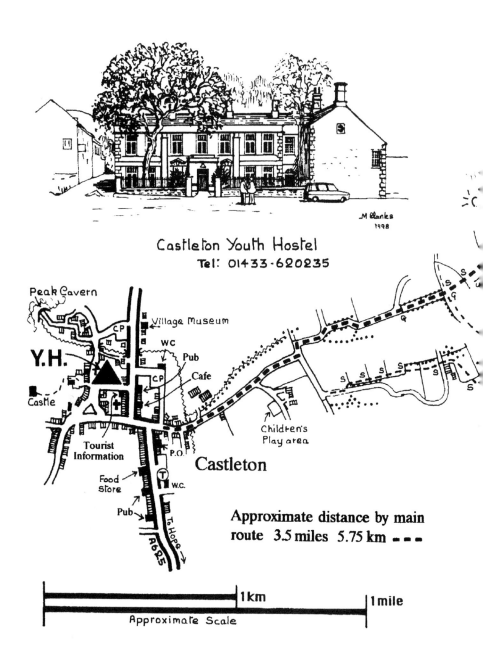

Castleton Youth Hostel
Tel: 01433·620235

Peak Cavern
Village Museum
C.P
WC
Pub
Y.H.
Cafe
C.P
Castle
Children's Play area
Tourist Information
P.O.
Castleton
Food Store
W.C.
Pub
To Hope
A625

Approximate distance by main route 3.5 miles 5.75 km ▬ ▬ ▬

1km | 1 mile

Approximate Scale

M Blanks
1998

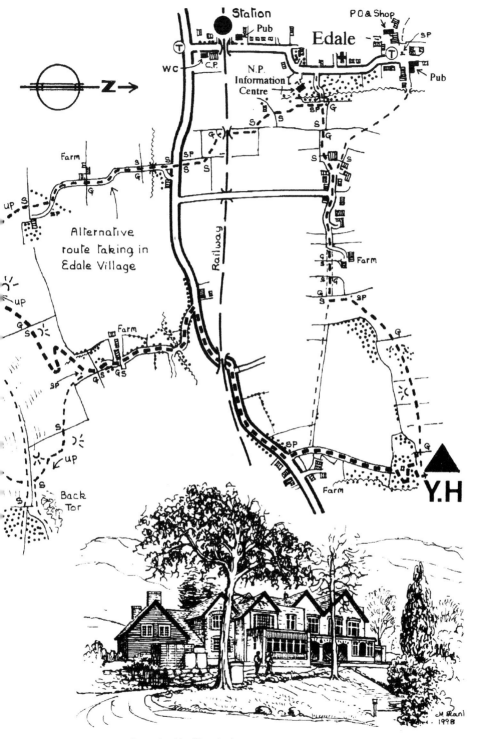

Edale Youth Hostel. Tel: 01433-670302

21

Map 5
Castleton YH to Hathersage YH: 1
see page 11

Approximate distance of main route - **Bretton** 7 miles 11 km
Eyam 8.5miles 13.5 km

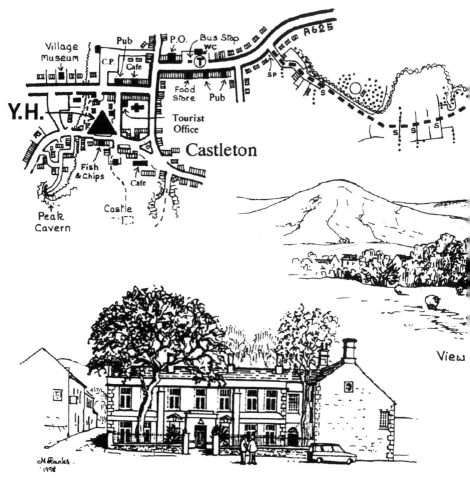

Castleton Youth Hostel
Tel: 01433-620235

1km | 1mile
Approximate Scale

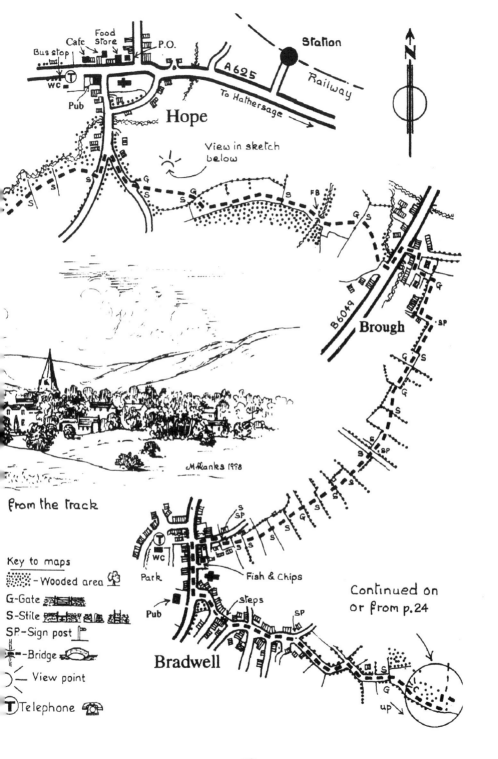

Food
store
Cafe
P.O.
Bus stop
WC
Pub
Hope
Station
A625
Railway
To Hathersage
N

View in sketch
below

S
S
S
G
S
G
FB
S
G
S

B6049
Brough
G
SP
G S
S
S
SP

M.Hanks 1998

From the track

Key to maps

⬛ - Wooded area 🌳
G - Gate
S - Stile
SP - Sign post
🌉 - Bridge
)(- View point
T - Telephone

S
SP
G
S
S
S
S
G
G
S
S
SP
S

T
WC
Park
Pub
Fish & Chips
steps
SP
Bradwell

Continued on
or from p.24

S
G
up

23

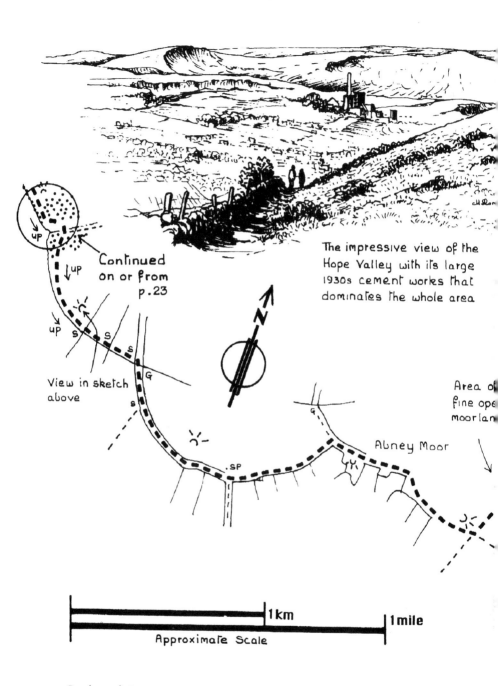

The impressive view of the Hope Valley with its large 1930s cement works that dominates the whole area

Continued on or from p.23

uP

↓uP

uP

View in sketch above

S   S   S

S

G

S

SP

Area of fine ope moorlan

G

Abney Moor

Y

N

1km

1mile

Approximate Scale

Designed by M Hanks.

Map 6
Castleton YH to Hathersage YH: 2
see page 11

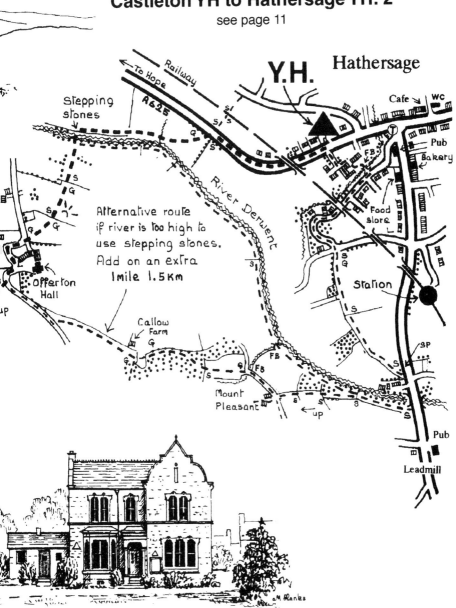

Railway
To Hope
A625
To Hope

Y.H. Hathersage

Stepping stones

Cafe WC

Pub

Bakery

Alternative route
if river is too high to
use stepping stones.
Add on an extra
1mile 1.5km

River Derwent

Food store

Offerton Hall

Station

Callow Farm

Mount Pleasant
up

FB
FB

up

SP

Pub

Leadmill

Hathersage Youth Hostel
Tel: 01433-650493

Map 7
Castleton YH to Bretton YH and Eyam YH: 1

see page 12

Approximate distance of main route - Bretton 7 miles 11 km
Eyam 8.5miles 13.5 km

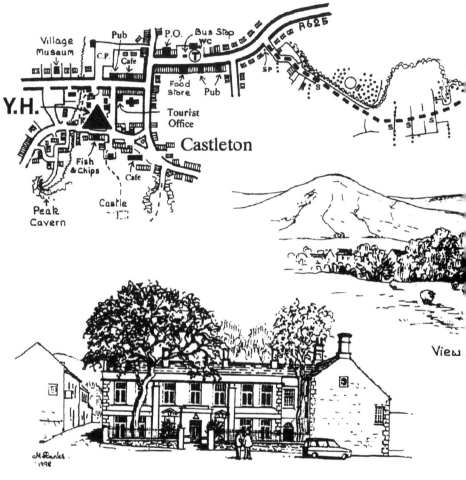

View

Castleton Youth Hostel
Tel: 01433-620235

1km   1mile
Approximate Scale

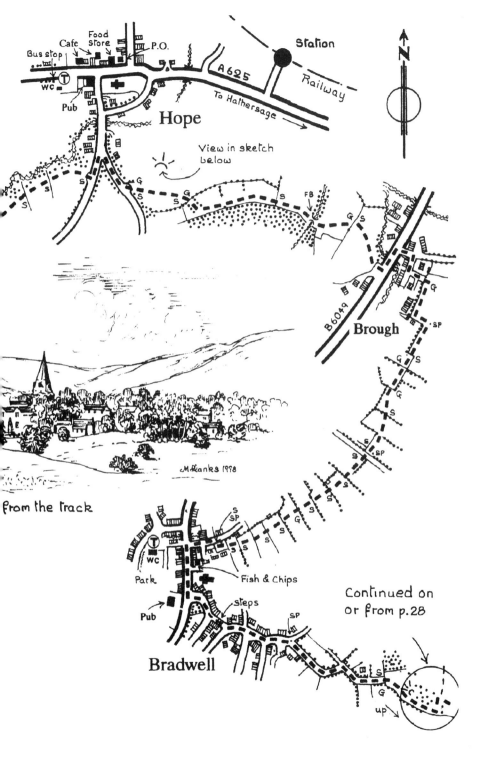

Bus stop
Cafe
Food Store
P.O.
Station
WC
Pub
Hope
A625
Railway
To Hathersage

View in sketch below

N

S
G
S
G
S
S
FB
G
S

Brough
B6049
G
SP
G
S
G
S
S
SP
S

from the track

M.Planks 1978

S
SP
G
S
S
S
S
G
S

WC
Park
Fish & Chips
Pub
steps
SP
Bradwell

G
S
G
up

Continued on or from p.28

Continued on
or from p. 27

Abney

Eyam Youth Hostel
Tel: 01433·630335

Y.H.
Bretto

Bretton Youth Hostel

Map 8
Castleton YH to Bretton YH and Eyam YH: 2
see page 12

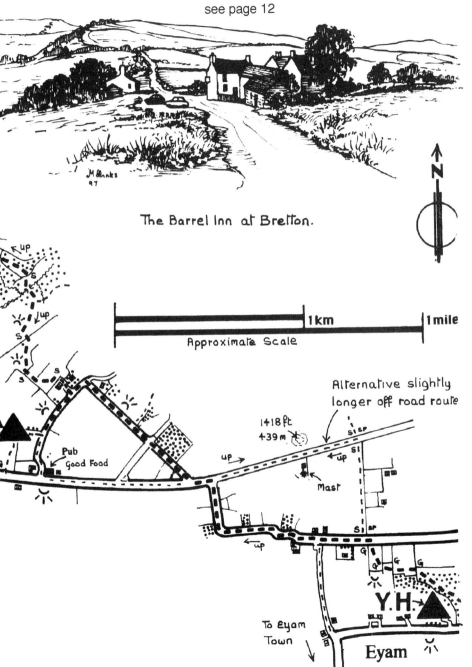

The Barrel Inn at Bretton.

N

up
S

up
S

S
S

Pub
Good Food

1418ft
439m

Alternative slightly
longer off road route

up

Mast

up

To Eyam
Town

Y.H.

Eyam

1km   1mile

Approximate Scale

29

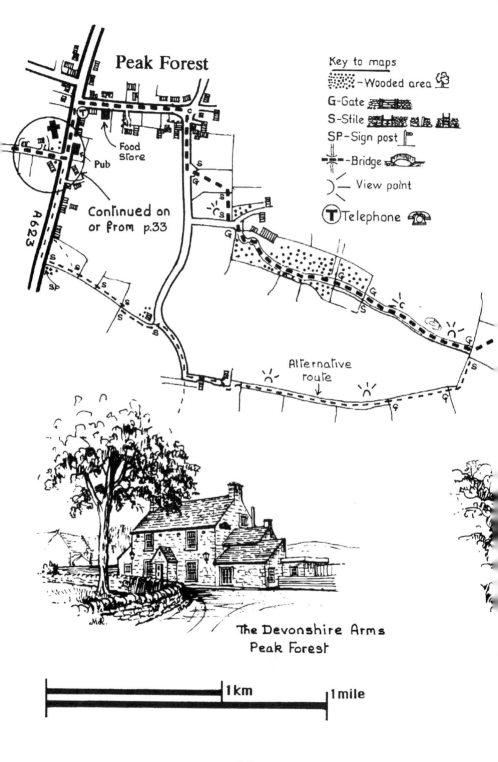

Peak Forest

Key to maps

- ░░░ — Wooded area 🌳
- G — Gate
- S — Stile
- SP — Sign post
- ╫ — Bridge
-))(— View point
- Ⓣ — Telephone ☎

Food store

Pub

Continued on or from p.33

A 623

Alternative route

The Devonshire Arms
Peak Forest

1 km   1 mile

Map 9
Castleton YH to Ravenstor YH: 1
see page 12

Approximate distance 9 miles   14.5 km

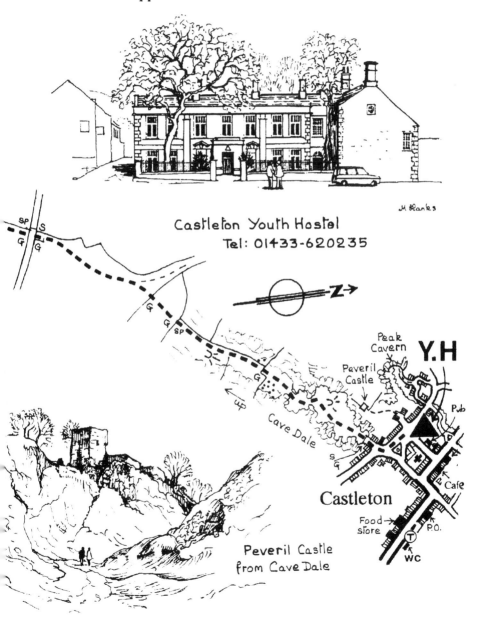

Castleton Youth Hostel
Tel: 01433-620235

Peak Cavern

Peveril Castle

Y.H

Pub

Cave Dale

Castleton

Cafe

Food store

P.O.

WC

Peveril Castle from Cave Dale

1

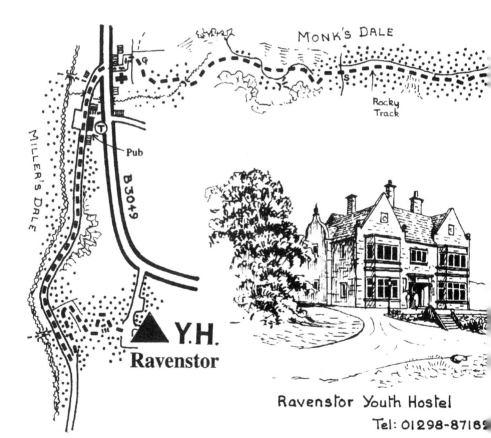

MONK'S DALE

MILLER'S DALE

B3049

Pub

Rocky Track

Y.H. Ravenstor

Ravenstor Youth Hostel
Tel: 01298-8718

Map 10
Castleton YH to Ravenstor YH: 2
see page 12

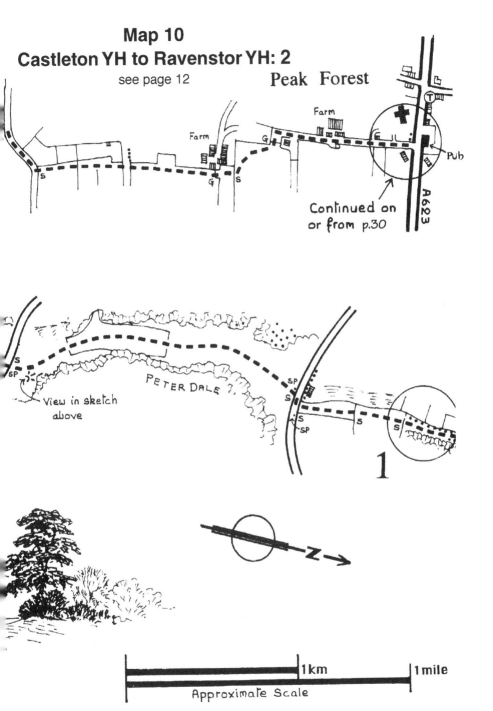

Peak Forest

Farm

Farm

Pub

A623

Continued on
or from p.30

PETER DALE

View in sketch
above

1

1km   1mile

Approximate Scale

Map 11
Edale, Mam Tor & Hollins Cross
see page 12

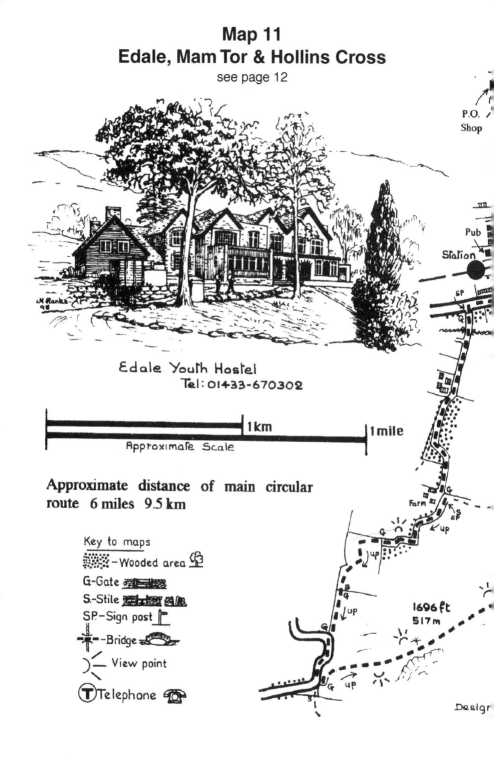

Edale Youth Hostel
Tel: 01433-670302

1km   1mile
Approximate Scale

Approximate distance of main circular
route 6 miles 9.5 km

Key to maps
░░░ – Wooded area
G-Gate
S.-Stile
SP.-Sign post
–Bridge
)ᴄ– View point
ⓣTelephone

P.O.
Shop

Pub

Station
SP

Farm
up

up

up

up

1696 ft
517 m

up

up

Design

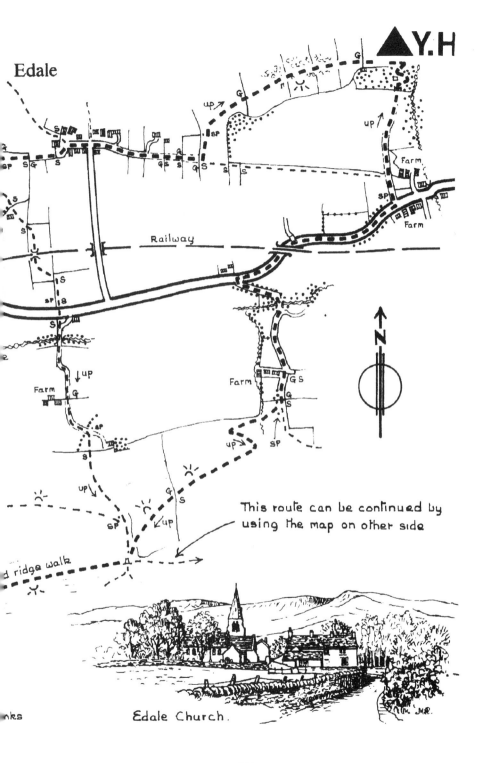

Edale

Y.H

Railway

This route can be continued by
using the map on other side

Edale Church.

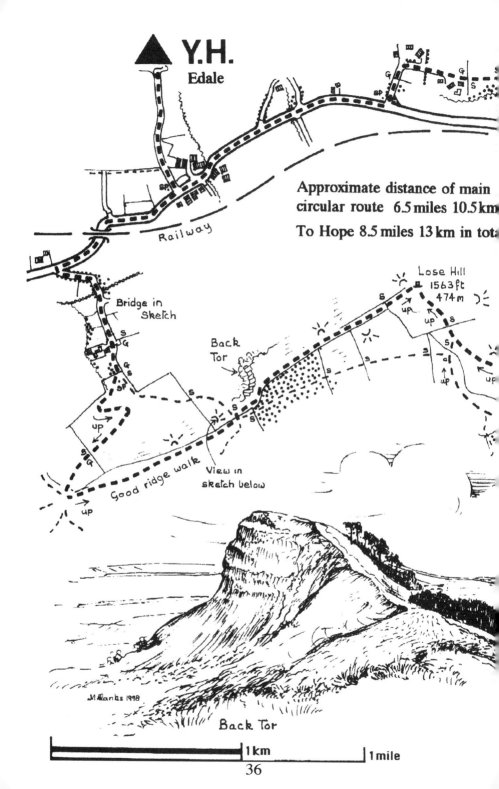

Y.H.
Edale

Approximate distance of main
circular route 6.5 miles 10.5 km

To Hope 8.5 miles 13 km in total

Railway

Lose Hill
1563 ft
474 m

Bridge in
Sketch

Back
Tor

up

Good ridge walk

View in
sketch below

up

M.Banks 1998

Back Tor

1 km

1 mile

Map 12
Hollins Cross, Lose Hill & Edale End

see page 13

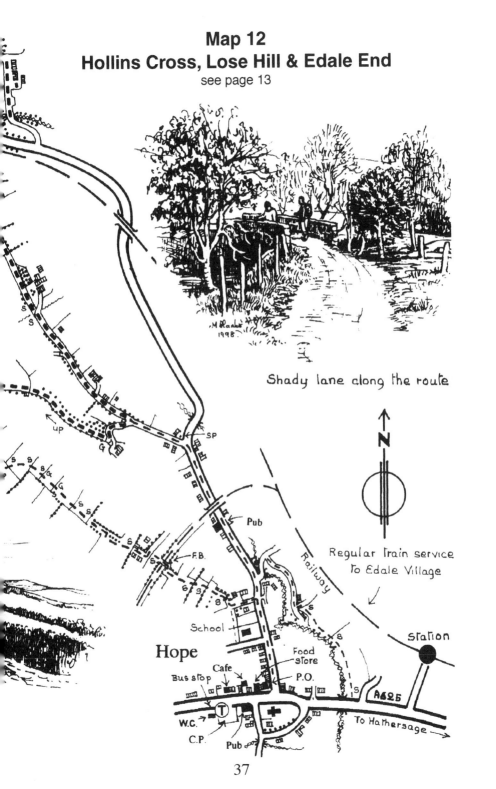

Shady lane along the route

N

Regular train service
to Edale Village

Pub

Railway

School

Hope

Food
store

Bus stop   Cafe

P.O.

Station

A625

W.C.

C.P.

Pub

To Hathersage

up

G

SP

F.B.

Map 13
Hathersage Village

Hathersage Youth Hostel
Tel: 01433-650493

Key to map
- Wooded area
- G-Gate
- S.-Stile
- SP.-Sign post
- Bridge
- View point
- Telephone

Hathersage Youth Hostel
Tel: 01433-650493

Royal
Bank of
Scotland

Y.H.→

Pub

A625

←To Hope

Railway

Foo
St

View in
sketch on rig

14th-Century Parish Church

Hostel stamp

Parish
Church

Baulk
Lane

Hathersage
Hall

Pub

Artist Supply
Shop

Pub

A 625

Pharmacy

age

N.W.
Bank

Hathersage

.P.

Swimming
pool

N

To
Sheffield

Station

B6001

Designed by M Hanks

39

Map 14
Hathersage to Stanage
see page 13

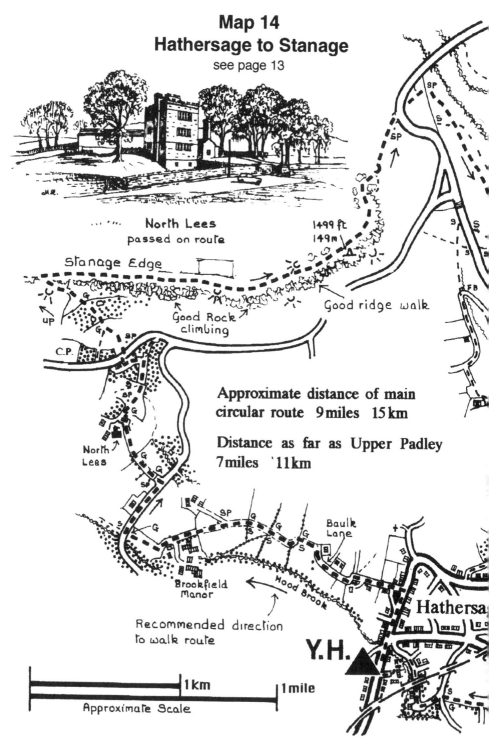

North Lees
passed on route

1499 ft
149m

Stanage Edge

Good ridge walk

Good Rock climbing

UP

C.P.

North Lees

Approximate distance of main circular route 9 miles 15 km

Distance as far as Upper Padley 7 miles 11 km

Baulk Lane

Brookfield Manor

Wood Brook

Hathersa

Recommended direction to walk route

Y.H.

1km

1 mile

Approximate Scale

40

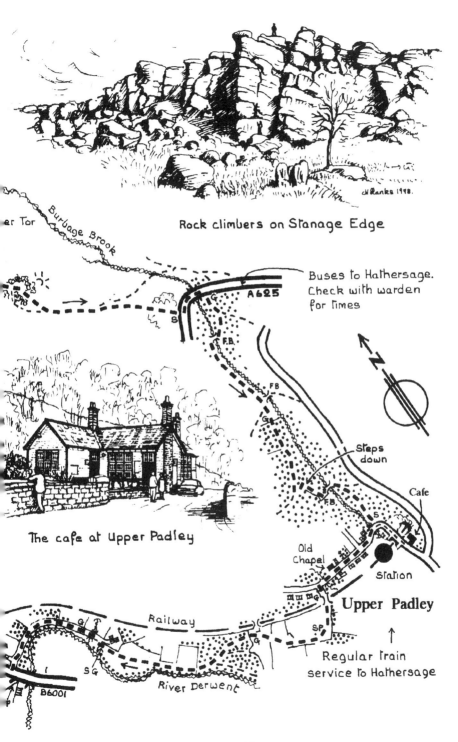

Rock climbers on Stanage Edge

Burbage Brook

er Tor

Buses to Hathersage.
Check with warden
for times

A625

F.B.

FB

Steps
down

Cafe

The cafe at Upper Padley

Old
Chapel

Station

Upper Padley

Railway

River Derwent

B6001

Regular train
service to Hathersage

Hathersage YH to Bretton YH & Eyam YH   (OS Outdoor Leisure Map 1 & 24)

Map 15 (see pages 46 / 47)   Bretton 5 miles (8km)   Eyam 5.5 miles (8.75km)

These are easy routes which climb up onto the moor (now a mixture of heath and fields) to reach Bretton and/or descend down into Eyam village. There are good views en-route.

Take the lane opposite the youth hostel under the railway and on down to the River Derwent. Cross the bridge and turn right along the lane before taking a path on the left, crossing the Highlow brook (a "low" is a burial mound). Upon reaching the road near Hazelford Hall, the paths diverge. If you are going to Bretton, turn right on the farm track which passes Tor Farm. The path continues across the fields above the valley of the Highlow Brook heading for Stolk Ford where Abney Clough meets Bretton Clough. Don't cross the bridge but take the path for Bretton Clough. It's well defined, climbing up and away from the brook. Upon reaching the top, the youth hostel is directly ahead, conveniently situated near to the Barrell Inn where you can have a pub meal instead of cooking for yourself at the hostel.

If you are heading for Eyam, walk up the road a short distance from Hazelford before turning right to climb up onto Eyam Moor. This is an old packhorse way and was in existence at least as early as 1791. Turn right on the disused road across Sir William Hill before turning left to drop down to Eyam YH.

Note the slightly longer path to Eyam via Stoke Ford. If you take this, a well defined path climbs up onto the moor once you reach Stoke Ford.

Hathersage YH to Edale YH   (OS Outdoor Leisure Map 1)

Map 16 / 17 (see pages 48 /51)   9 miles (14km)

This path heads for the River Derwent before climbing up to the top of Win Hill west of Ladybower Reservoir, and then slowly descending via Hope Cross to the Vale of Edale.

From the rear of the hostel, take the lane to Thorpe Farm (it is a Viking word, meaning small settlement or village). Cross the golf course to reach a small wood before descending into Bamford and heading for Bamford Mill. The old steam engine here is preserved and the mill premises are being converted to residential use.

Cross the River Derwent and climb up to Thornhill village. The path skirts the north-side before heading up a ridge to reach Win Hill Plantation.

Turn left to climb to the top of Win Hill before descending the ridge down to Hope Cross. If you wish to avoid the hilltop, you can skirt the east side of the hill on a path which runs along the top-edge of the wood. Either path brings you to an old Roman road ascending from Hope. It is the road from Anavio near Hope to the Roman fort at Glossop, heading for Doctor's Gate over the Snake Pass.

From Hope Cross, the path descends to the Vale of Edale and into Jagger's Clough. A jagger was the man in charge of a packhorse team. A well trodden path follows the valley side to reach the youth hostel. This path has some memorable views, so take the camera!

Walks around Eyam   (OS Outdoor Leisure Map 24)

Eyam to Stoney Middleton   4.5 miles (8km)
Map 18 (see pages 52 / 53)

This short route goes straight to the next village, Stoney Middleton, a couple of miles away. Whilst there, take a look at the unusual design of the church and the bath house of 1815. The path returns by the same route. Once back in Eyam, if you have time, take the road to your right past the cafe and out of the village. Follow it past the council houses and turn left up the farm track. Carry straight on at the top of the wood and you soon arrive at the Riley Graves. Here lie seven members of the Hancock family who died of the plague. Return by the same route to the village. It adds just over a mile to the journey.

Eyam to Foolow, Bretton YH & Eyam Moor   (OS Outdoor Leisure Map 24)
Map 19 (see pages 54 / 55)   7 miles (11km)

This route follows the routes described from Ravenstor to Eyam/Bretton and Hathersage to Eyam/ Bretton. It is perhaps best to head for Eyam Moor first, crossing the moor on a well defined path before descending to Stoke Ford. Don't cross the footbridge, but turn left and walk up Bretton Clough to reach Bretton, with its little youth hostel and pub — The Barrel.

Descend by road to Foolow where there is another pub — The Bulls Head. Have a look around the green with its pond, cross, manor and bullring. From here a path cuts through the fields back to Eyam. There are lovely views across the moor and from Bretton.

This walk doubles as a route between Eyam YH and Bretton YH. If you are going to take a packed lunch, go to Stoke Ford. If you want a pub lunch, go to Foolow, perhaps taking in a look around Eyam village before you start the walk in either case. The distance to Bretton is short whichever route you take.

Eyam YH to Bretton YH
This route is covered under **Walks around Eyam**

Walks around Bretton   (OS Outdoor Leisure Map 24)
Bretton to Abney & Bretton Clough   4 miles (6.5km)
Map 20   (see pages 56 / 57)

Turn up the back lane before going through a gate to descend into Bretton Clough. It is a fairly well-wooded area, the path dropping pleasantly down to Stoke Ford. Cross the footbridge and then walk up Abney Clough to the hamlet of Abney. Turn left upon reaching the road and then left again to head for Cockey Farm. The path descends down into Bretton Clough before climbing out to reach the lane behind the youth hostel.

The youth hostel stands on the southern edge of a huge moorland area drained diagonally by the Abney and Bretton Brooks (called Highlow Brook below Stoke Ford). This is easily appreci- ated from the area behind Bretton.

Walks around Ravenstor   (OS Outdoor Leisure Map 24)
Ravenstor to Monsal Head   7miles (11km)
Map 21   (see pages 58 / 59)

A walk with lovely surroundings and views. From the hostel grounds, descend into Miller's Dale and walk through Litton Mill to join the river. The latter backs up behind a weir as you approach Cressbrook Dale — the valley is known as Water-cum-Jolly Dale. By Sir Richard Arkwright's

Cressbrook Mill, turn right, but look to your left to see an unusually designed building. It was the apprentices' house for the mill.

Tideswell and Miller's Dale
Map 22 (see page 60 / 61)

Climb uphill to reach the old Midland Railway's Buxton-Bakewell line, now the Monsal Trail. Stay on this until you reach the huge Monsal viaduct (see illustration on map). Here you can cross the bridge and climb out of the valley to the pub and cafe at Monsal Head. Alternatively, or after your refreshments, walk down the valley before climbing up to Brushfield House. An easier climb out of the valley on a farm road is available.

Upon reaching the top of the valley side, it is an easy stroll along lanes and through fields before, once again, you are standing on the edge of the valley. The view is stunning and the youth hostel can be seen way below you. Descend to the Monsal Trail where you cross the bridge and drop down to Litton Mill or turn left and walk along the Trail before descending to the river opposite the youth hostel.

Ravenstor to Tideswell and Cressbrook Dale   (OS Outdoor Leisure Map 24)
Map 21   (see pages 62 / 65)   6.5 miles (10.5km)

Drop down through the youth hostel garden to Tideswell Dale, turn left and walk up the valley. You pass an old quarry, and a beech tree avenue which was the quarry entrance. Proceed into Tideswell village. The church is known as the Cathedral of the Peak. It is Early English in style in the chancel, but the rebuilding took so long that the west end is Perpendicular.

Just past the Rock & Mineral shop, turn right and follow the lane to Litton (look out for the stocks). Cut across the fields to descend into Cressbrook Dale and turn right for Cressbrook. Years ago, peppermint used to be grown in the valley for commercial purposes. Leave the valley for the village and then descend to Litton Mill and the short distance back to Ravenstor.

Ravenstor YH to Bretton YH & Eyam YH   (OS Outdoor Leisure Map 24)
Maps 23 / 24 (see pages 62 / 65)   Eyam 7 miles (11km)   Bretton 6 miles(9.5km)

This route heads for the Derbyshire plateau, leaving the dales behind to cross fields bounded by dry stone walls. From the youth hostel, head down into Miller's Dale to reach Litton Mill. Turn left to climb out of the Dale for Cressbrook and the Dale of the same name. The stream dries up to create a "dry dale" which heads for the A623 at Wardlow Mires. It passes a limestone outcrop called Peter's Stone which is quite a pronounced feature.

From the Three Stags pub, turn left and head across the fields to Foolow village. The village has an attractive green with its manor house, well, duckpond, 14th-century cross and bull-baiting stone. The Bulls Head Inn serves food until 2pm. Between Wardlow and Foolow the path takes you over the limestone plateau. Ahead is the escarpment of Eyam Edge, where the limestone is covered by gritstones and moorland prevails. Leaving Foolow for Eyam, a series of small fields are crossed with Eyam Edge to your left. Following the earlier lead mining activities in this area, the more valuable fluorspar is now quarried, and processed at Cavendish Mill to the south of Eyam.

The latter village is famous for the plague which devastated the village in 1665/66. In all, 257 villagers died. There is a Museum of the Plague in the village opposite the car park / WC in Hawkhill Road. The latter rises up the hillside to the youth hostel. The church is well worth a visit and it has an impressive Celtic Cross. Nearby is Eyam Hall, built fifty years after the plague and now open to the public. There is much to see around Eyam.

If you are heading to Bretton from Foolow, take the lane past the chapel and climb slowly up the hillside to Bretton and the hostel. The pub — The Barrel — serves food and is used to a regular trade from hostellers! There are splendid views from Eyam Edge down onto the limestone plateau and across the moors towards Kinder Scout and the Eastern Moors.

Ravenstor YH to Buxton YH

Maps 25 / 26 (see pages 66 / 69)

(OS Outdoor Leisure Map 24)

8 miles (12.75km)

A route crossing the limestone plateau just south of the River Wye.

Descend down the old drive opposite the youth hostel steps, to the River Wye. Cross the latter and climb up the steep side of Monsal Dale. The view from the top rewards the effort; the walking is then fairly flat along farm tracks and across fields to Taddington. Head for the church steeple, before climbing out of the village onto South Top. The path then follows a wall before dropping down into Chelmorton.

From above the village, you can see an incredible number of medieval strip fields. Prior to the Enclosures, villagers were alloted 2 or 3 strips together with a frontage to the village street. Houses were built on the plot frontage but the outline of the old strip system remains preserved in all the walls. The church is one of the highest in the county and has a collection of stone coffins carved with various motifs.

From the village, take the lane heading for Deep Dale, a dry dale which formerly drained towards the River Wye. Continue across the fields through the hamlet of Cow Dale before reaching the outskirts of Buxton and the large railway viaduct of the former line to Ashbourne. It was built around 1890. Walk under the viaduct, the youth hostel is ahead.

Walks around Buxton

(OS Outdoor Leisure Map 24)

Buxton to Poole's Cavern and Solomon's Temple

Map 27 (see page 70 / 71)

Buxton has a large country park of well over a 100 acres. It is chiefly wooded and has two principal attractions: Poole's Cavern — the prettiest limestone cave in the Peak; and Solomon's Temple — a folly now restored and offering superb views to the western moors and over the rolling limestone plateau with its drystone walls. It is only a short walk to the Park from the youth hostel. Note that, at least a mile away, the Safeway Store is alot further from the YH than the map would suggest. Refill your empty water bottles at St Anne's Well — opposite The Crescent — it's free Buxton Mineral water!

Buxton, Harpur Hill and Deep Dale

(OS Outdoor Leisure Map 24)

Map 28 (see page 72 / 73)

7 miles (11km)

Take the path up the valley west of Harpur Hill Road until the road to Leek is reached. Turn left and walk through the village to Haslin Road, opposite the large High Peak College. Turn right and join the old Cromford & High Peak Railway for a short distance before reaching the section which is still railed for quarry traffic. Turn left under the railway and head for Brierlow Bar to cross the A515. The path then enters Back Dale, which is very shallow at first, gradually deepening and changing its name to Deep Dale.

Upon reaching the old way from Buxton to Chelmorton, join this path, turning left and climbing out of the dale. The path runs straight back to the hostel via the hamlet of Cow Dale.

This is a quiet path, compensating for some road walking through Harpur Hill.

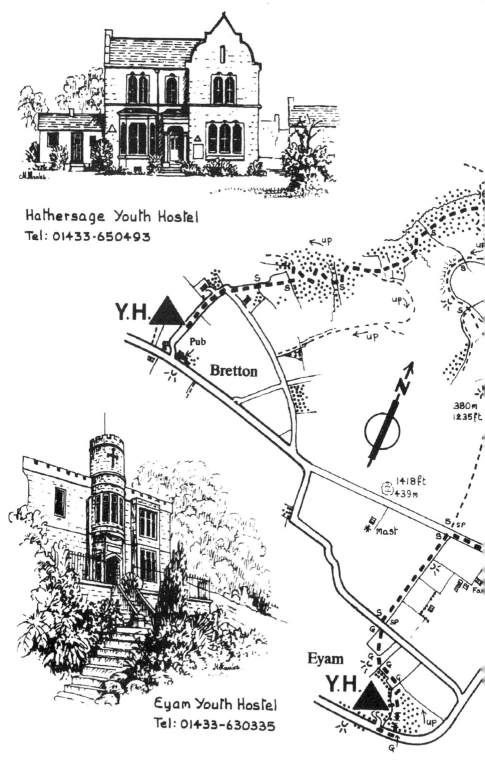

Hathersage Youth Hostel
Tel: 01433·650493

Bretton

Pub

Y.H.

Eyam Youth Hostel
Tel: 01433-630335

Eyam

Y.H.

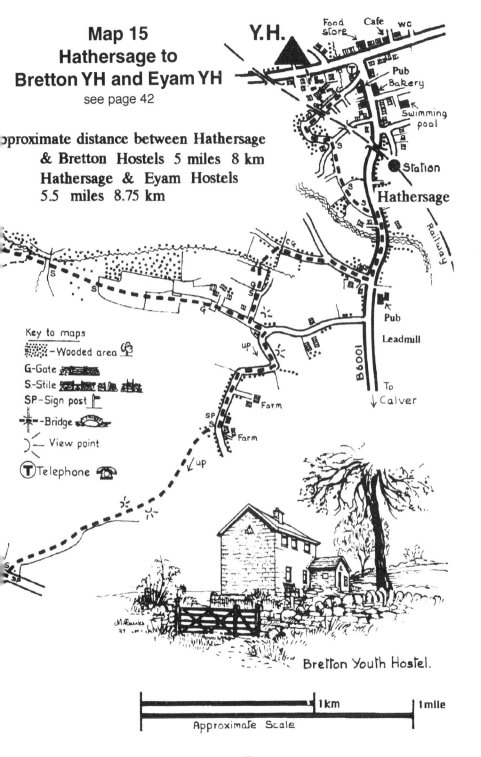

Map 15
Hathersage to
Bretton YH and Eyam YH
see page 42

pproximate distance between Hathersage
& Bretton Hostels 5 miles 8 km
Hathersage & Eyam Hostels
5.5 miles 8.75 km

Y.H.

Food store Cafe WC

Pub
Bakery

Swimming pool

Station

Hathersage

Railway

CG

Pub

Leadmill

B6001

To
↓ Calver

UP

Farm

SP
S

Farm

up

Key to maps
- Wooded area
G-Gate
S.-Stile
SP-Sign post
-Bridge
) - View point
(T) Telephone

S
SP

Bretton Youth Hostel.

1km   1 mile
Approximate Scale

47

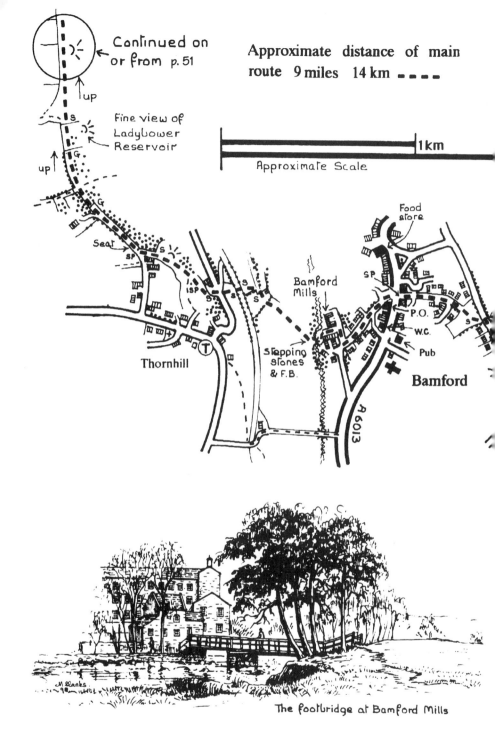

Continued on
or from p. 51

up

s

Fine view of
Ladybower
Reservoir

G

up

G

Approximate distance of main
route 9 miles   14 km ▪ ▬ ▬ ▬

1km

Approximate Scale

Seat

SP

s

S

SP

SP

s

S

Food
store

P

SP

P.O.

W.C.

Bamford
Mills

s

Thornhill

T

Stepping
Stones
& F.B.

Pub

Bamford

A 6013

The footbridge at Bamford Mills

M. Banks

48

Map 16
Hathersage YH to Edale YH: 1
See page 42

le

Hathersage Youth Hostel
Te: 01433-650493

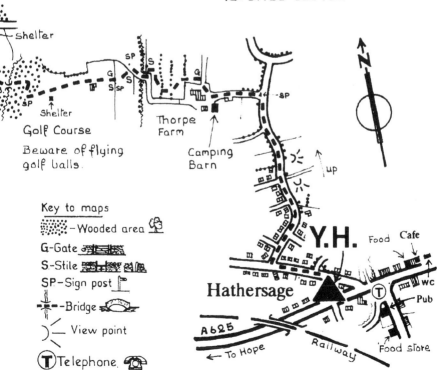

shelter

Golf Course

Beware of flying
golf balls.

Thorpe
Farm

Camping
Barn

up

Key to maps

░ - Wooded area 🌳

G-Gate ▦▦

S-Stile ▦▦

SP-Sign post

▪-▪-Bridge

)⁚- View point

(T) Telephone. ☎

Y.H.   Food Cafe

Hathersage   wc

Pub

A625

← To Hope   Railway   Food store

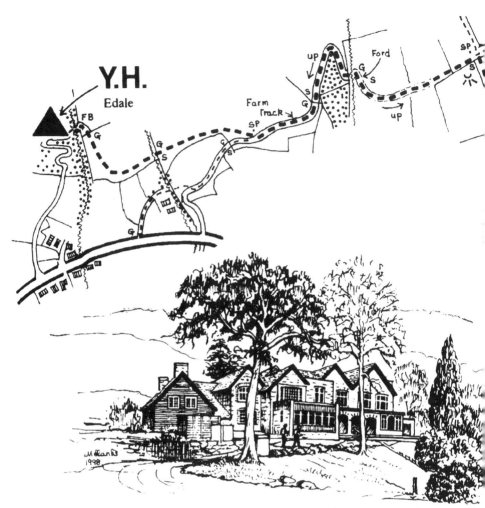

Edale Youth Hostel

Track leading up from Edale
Towards Winhill Pike

Map 17
Hathersage YH to Edale YH: 2
See page 42

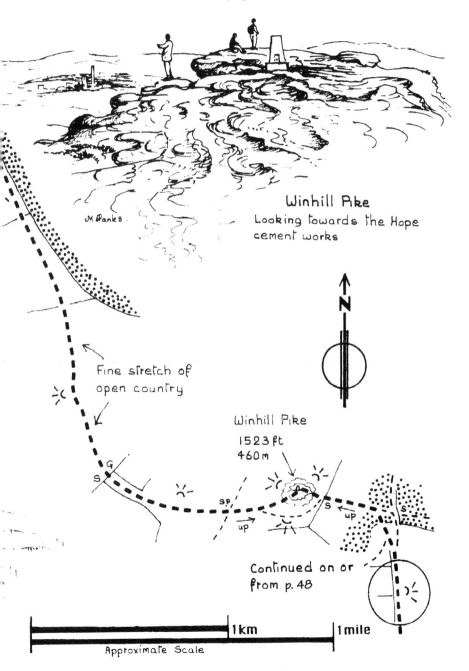

Winhill Pike

Looking towards the Hope
cement works

M.Danks

N

Fine stretch of
open country

Winhill Pike

1523 ft
460 m

G

S

sp

up

up

S

up

S

Continued on or
from p. 48

1 km   1 mile

Approximate Scale

51

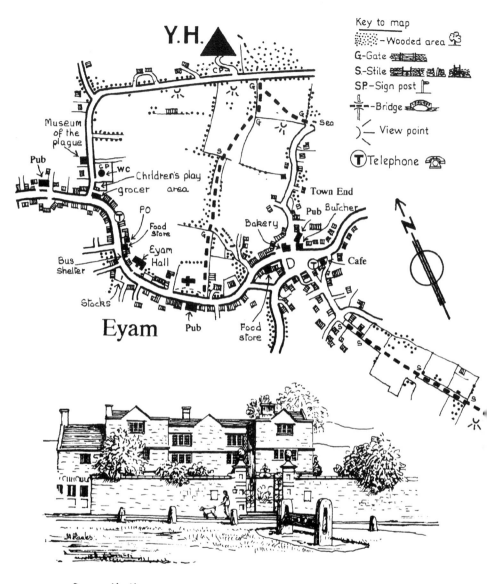

Key to map

- :::: – Wooded area
- G - Gate
- S - Stile
- SP - Sign post
- Bridge
- View point
- (T) Telephone

Y.H.

CP

Museum of the plague

Pub

CP WC

Children's play area

grocer

PO

Food store

Bus Shelter

Eyam Hall

Stocks

Eyam

Pub

Food store

Town End

Pub Butcher

Bakery

Cafe

Sea

Eyam Hall.
   Open Wed, Thur & Sun 11AM to 4·30PM.

Approximate Scale

1km

0.5 miles

Map 18
Eyam to Stoney Middleton
see page 42

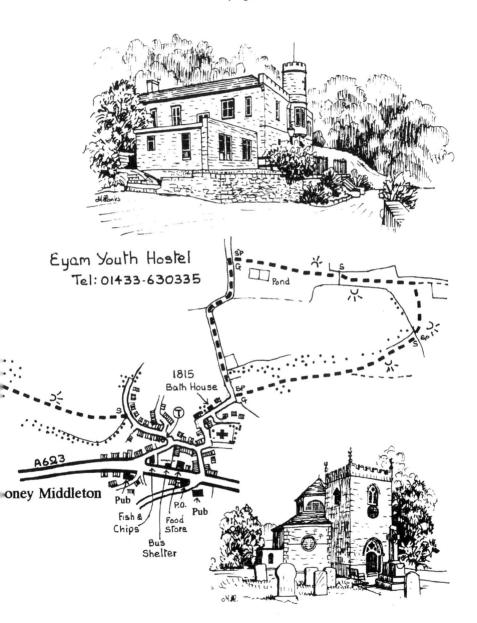

Eyam Youth Hostel
Tel: 01433-630335

Pond

1815
Bath House

A623

oney Middleton

Pub

Fish &
Chips

P.O.

Food
Store

Pub

Bus
Shelter

Stoney Middleton Church.

Map 19
Eyam to Foolow, Bretton YH and Eyam Moor
see page 43

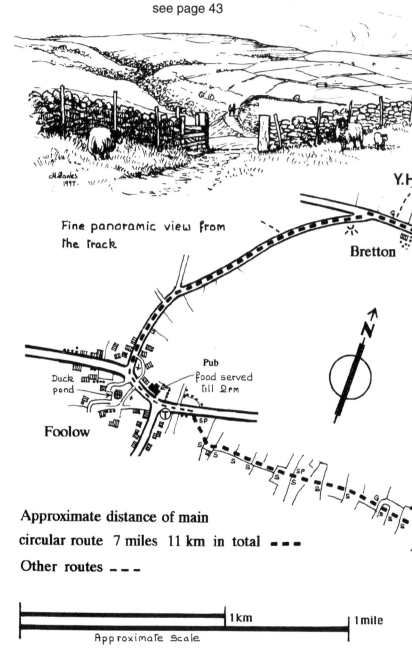

M. Danks 1997.

Y.H.

Fine panoramic view from the track.

Bretton

N

Pub
Food served till 2pm

Duck pond

Foolow

SP

S S S S

S S

SP

S S

S G S

S

Approximate distance of main circular route 7 miles 11 km in total ▬ ▬ ▬

Other routes _ _ _

1 km

1 mile

Approximate Scale

54

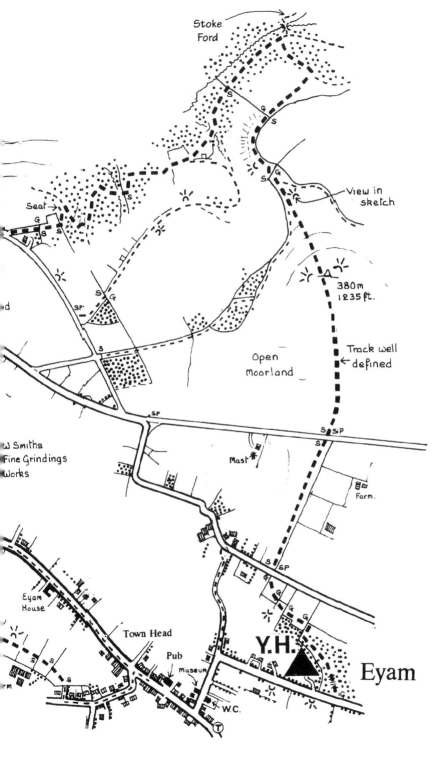

Stoke Ford

Seat

View in sketch

380m
1235ft.

Track well
← defined

Open
moorland

d

SP

ω Smiths
Fine Grindings
Works

Mast

Farm.

Eyam
House

Town Head

Pub

Museum

W.C.

Y.H.

Eyam

55

Map 20
Bretton to Abney and Bretton Clough
see page 43

Bretton Youth Hostel

Key to maps
- ░░░ -Wooded area 🍀
- G.-Gate ▦▦
- S.-Stile ▦▦
- S.P.-Sign post ⌐
- ⊹-Bridge ◠
-)ͼ View point
- (T)Telephone ☎

Approximate distance of main circular route 4 miles 6.5 km ▬ ▬ ▬

Other routes ‒ ‒ ‒ ‒

See also Map 19 for more walks

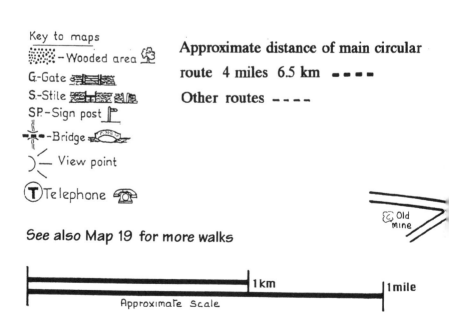

🐛 Old mine

1 km	1 mile

Approximate Scale

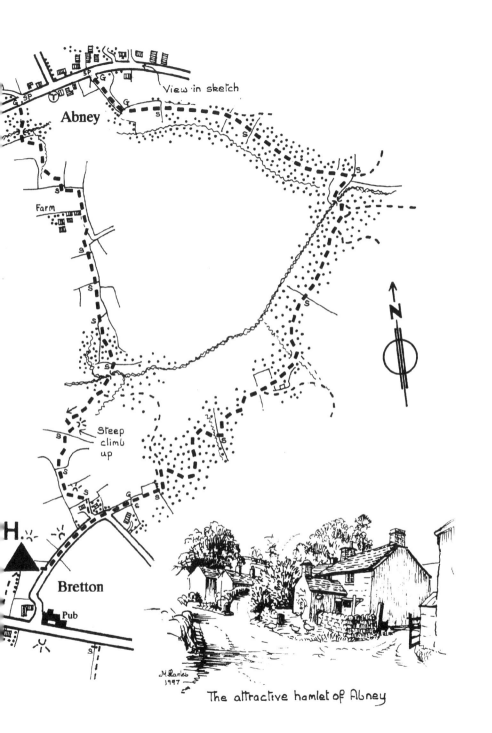

View in sketch

Abney

Farm

↑
N

← Steep
climb
up

H

Bretton

Pub

The attractive hamlet of Abney

M.Lanes
1997

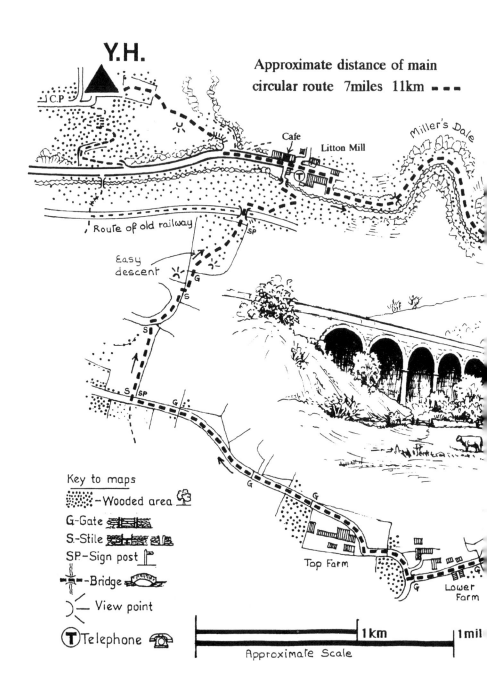

Y.H.

C.P

Approximate distance of main
circular route 7miles 11km ■ ■ ■

Miller's Dale

Cafe
Litton Mill

Route of old railway

Easy
descent

SP

G
S

S

S SP
G

Top Farm

G

G

Lower
Farm
G

G

Key to maps

▒▒ —Wooded area

G-Gate

S.-Stile

SP.-Sign post

▬╫▬ -Bridge

)(— View point

(T)Telephone

1km   1mil

Approximate Scale

58

Map 21
Ravenstor to Monsal Head
see page 43 / 44

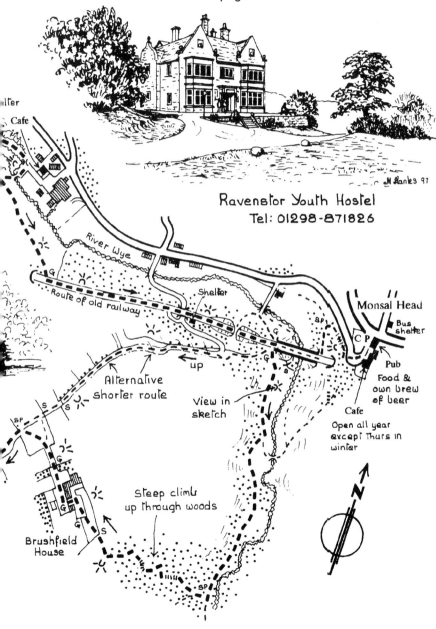

Ravenstor Youth Hostel
Tel: 01298-871826

Cafe

River Wye

G

Route of old railway

Shelter

Monsal Head

SP

Bus shelter

C P

Pub
Food &
own brew
of beer

Cafe

Open all year
except Thurs in
winter

up

Alternative
shorter route

View in
sketch

s s

SP

G

Steep climb
up through woods

Brushfield
House

G

S

SP

59

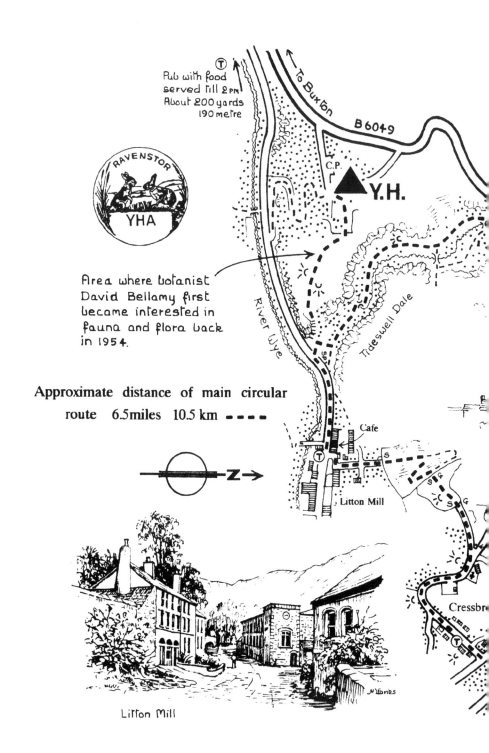

Pub with food
served till 2 PM
About 200 yards
190 metre

To Buxton

B 6049

C.P.

Y.H.

Tideswell Dale

River Wye

RAVENSTOR
YHA

Area where botanist
David Bellamy first
became interested in
fauna and flora back
in 1954.

**Approximate distance of main circular
route   6.5miles   10.5 km - - - -**

Z →

Cafe

Litton Mill

Cressbr

Litton Mill

60

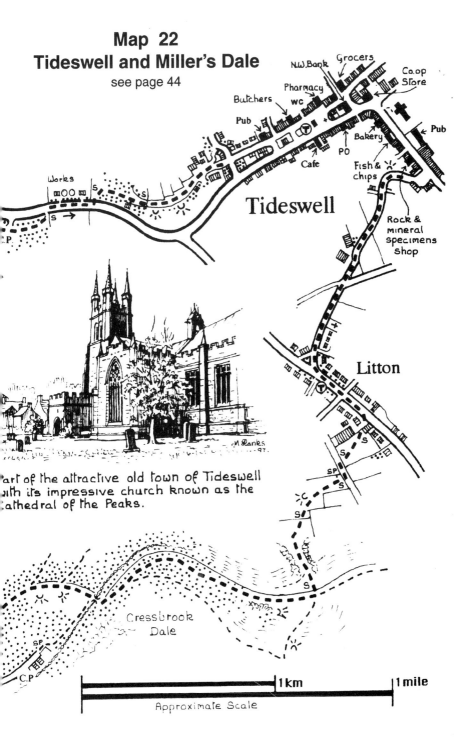

Map 22
Tideswell and Miller's Dale
see page 44

N.W. Bank
Grocers
Co.op Store
Pharmacy
Butchers
wc
Pub
Bakery
Pub
PO
Cafe
Fish & chips
Works
Tideswell
Rock & mineral specimens Shop
P
Litton
SP
S
C
S
art of the attractive old town of Tideswell ith its impressive church known as the athedral of the Peaks.

SP
C.P

Cressbrook Dale

1 km   1 mile
Approximate Scale

61

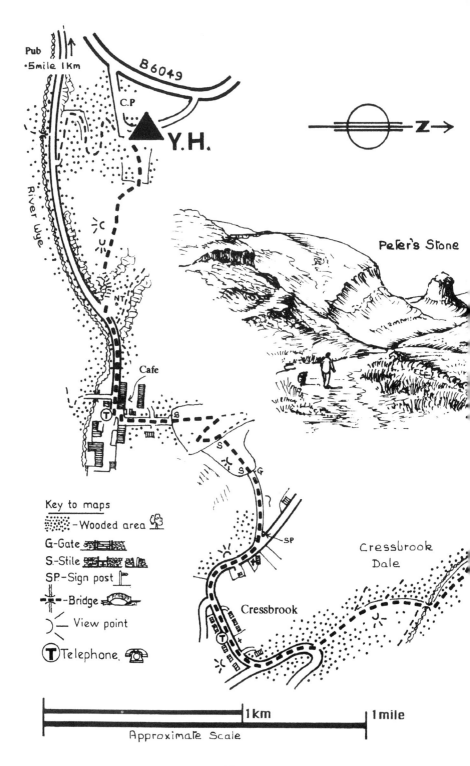

Pub
·5mile 1Km

B6049

C.P

Y.H.

River Wye

Peter's Stone

Cafe

Key to maps
:::: – Wooded area
G–Gate
S.–Stile
SP–Sign post
–Bridge
View point
(T) Telephone.

Cressbrook
Dale

SP

Cressbrook

Z→

1km   1mile

Approximate Scale

62

Map 23
Ravenstor to Bretton YH and Eyam YH: 1
see page 44

Ravenstor Youth Hostel
Tel: 01298-871826

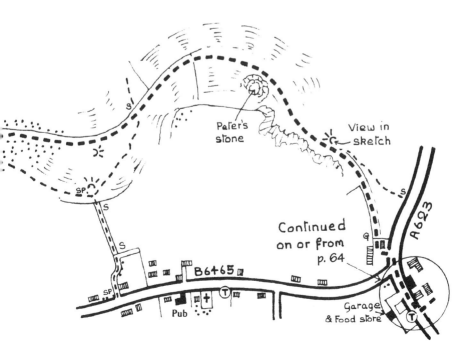

Map 24
Ravenstor to Bretton YH and Eyam YH: 2
see page 44

Approximate distance of main routes
Ravenstor / Eyam 7 miles 11km
Ravenstor / Bretton 6 miles 9.5km

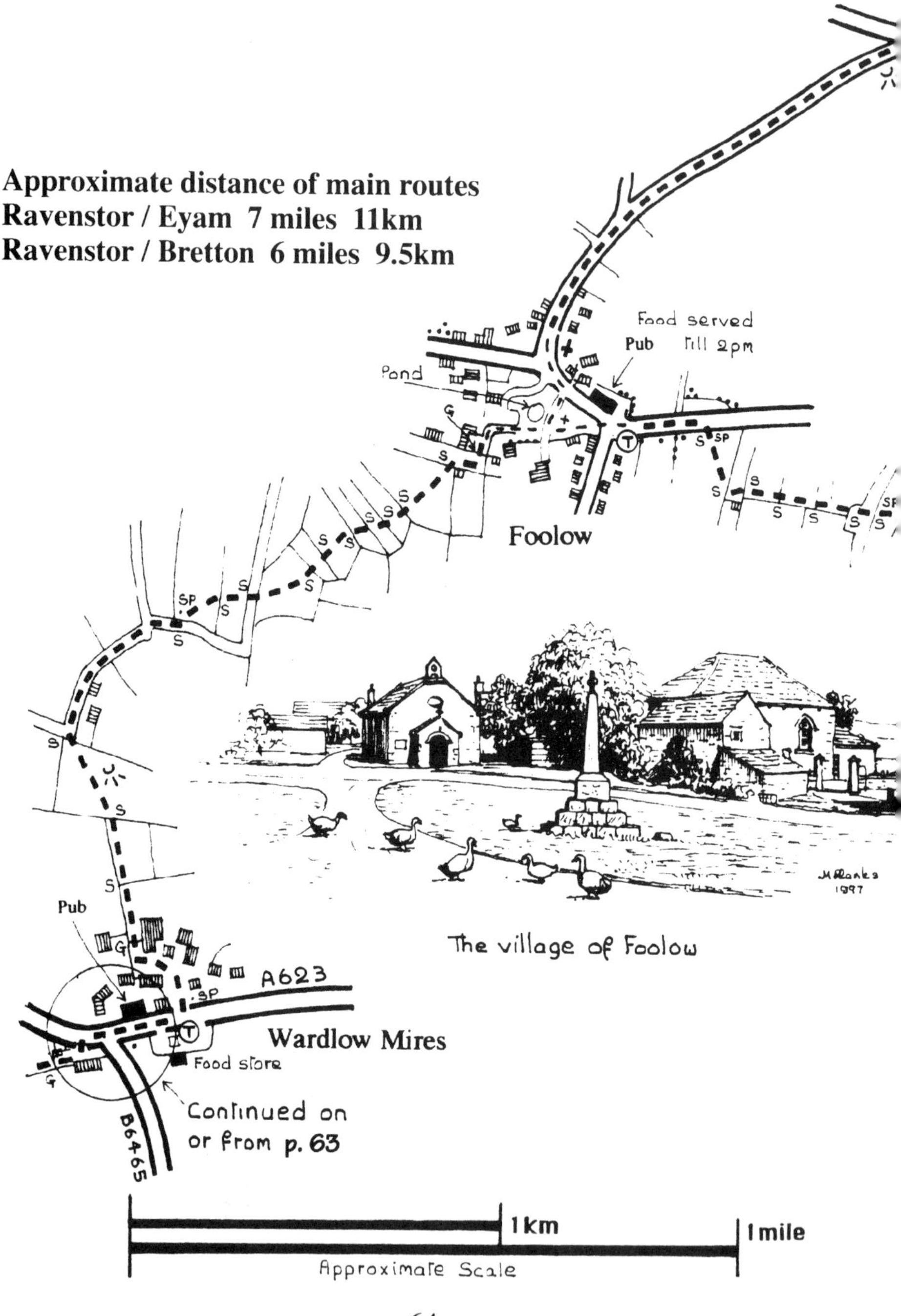

Food served
Pub Till 2pm

Pond

Foolow

SP

SP

The village of Foolow

M Ranks
1997

Pub

A623

Wardlow Mires

Food store

Continued on
or from p. 63

B6465

| 1 km | 1 mile |

Approximate Scale

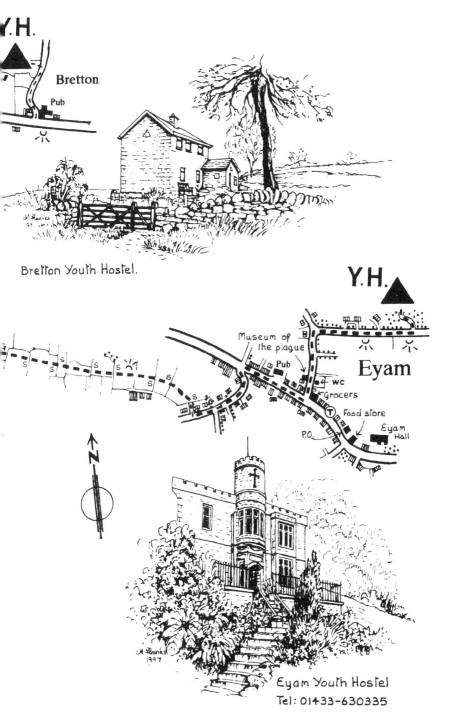

Bretton Youth Hostel.

Y.H.

Bretton

Pub

Museum of
the plague

Pub

Eyam

wc
Grocers

Food store

P.O.

Eyam
Hall

N

Eyam Youth Hostel
Tel: 01433-630335

Map 25
Ravenstor YH to Buxton YH: 1
see page 45

Ravenstor Youth Hostel
Tel: 01298-871826

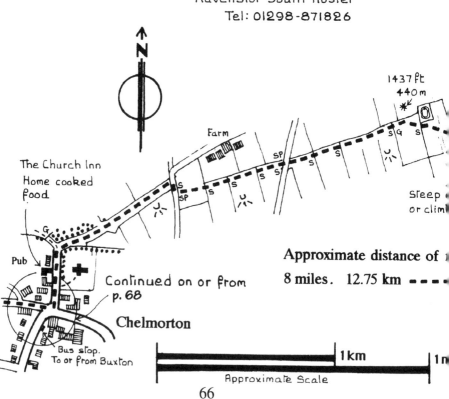

1437 ft
440 m

Farm

The Church Inn
Home cooked
food

Pub

Steep
or climb

Continued on or from
p. 68

Chelmorton

Approximate distance of
8 miles. 12.75 km - - - -

Bus stop.
To or from Buxton

1 km

1 m

Approximate Scale

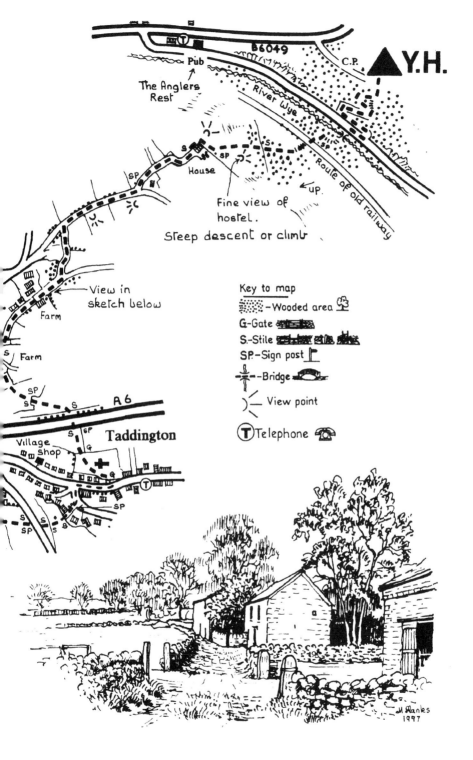

B6049

Pub

The Anglers Rest

C.P.

Y.H.

River Wye

Route of old railway

up.

Fine view of hostel.
Steep descent or climb

S

SP

House

SP

View in sketch below

Farm

Farm

S

SP

S

S

A6

Taddington

SP

G

Village Shop

G

G

T

SP

S

S

S

SP

Key to map

- Wooded area

G-Gate

S.-Stile

SP-Sign post

- Bridge

- View point

T Telephone

M Planks
1997

Map 26
Ravenstor YH to Buxton YH: 2
see page 45

Buxton Youth Hostel
Tel· 01298·22287

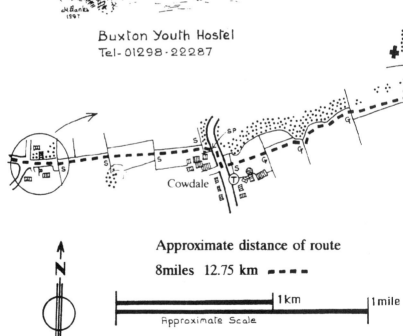

Cowdale

Approximate distance of route

8miles 12.75 km ▬ ▬ ▬ ▬

N

|1km |1mile
Approximate Scale

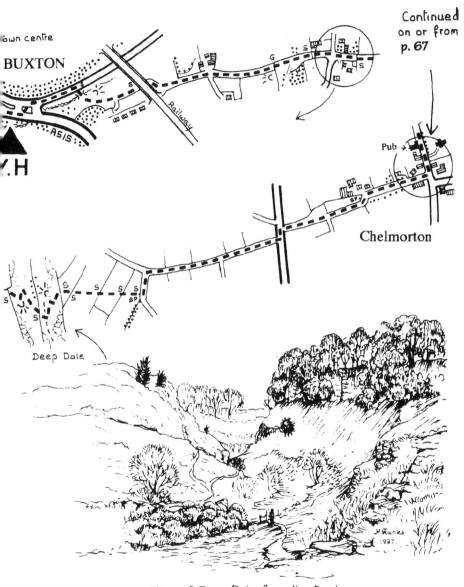

Continued on or from p. 67

BUXTON

Y.H

Pub

Chelmorton

Deep Dale

View of Deep Dale from the Track.

Map 27
Buxton to Poole's Cavern and Solomon's Temple
see page 45

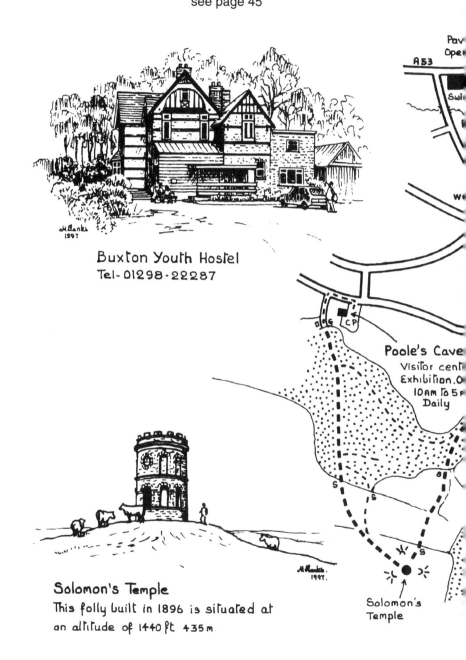

Buxton Youth Hostel
Tel- 01298-22287

A53

Pav
Ope

Swi

W

Poole's Cave
Visitor cent
Exhibition.O
10am to 5p
Daily

CP

Solomon's
Temple

Solomon's Temple
This folly built in 1896 is situated at
an altitude of 1440 ft 435 m.

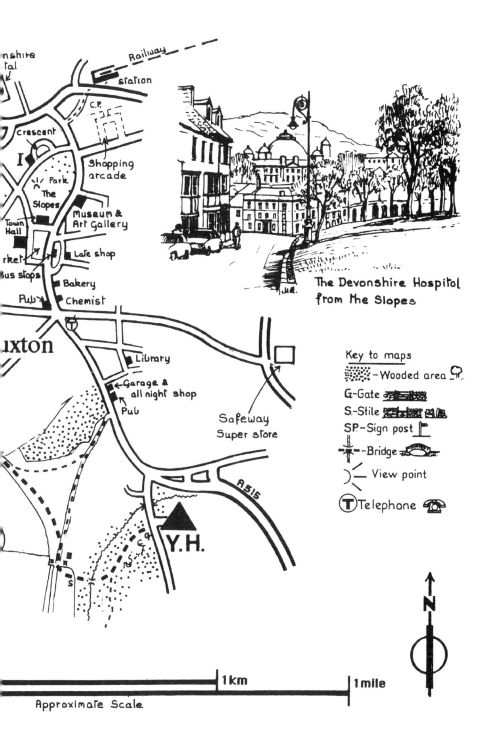

Railway

nshire
ral

station

C.P.

Crescent

I

Park
The
Slopes

Shopping
arcade

Museum &
Art Gallery

Town
Hall

rket

Cafe shop

us stops

Bakery

Pub

Chemist

ⓣ

ıxton

Library

Garage &
all night shop

Pub

Safeway
Super store

A515

△ Y.H.

S

The Devonshire Hospital
from the Slopes

Key to maps

▓ –Wooded area 🌳

G–Gate ▨▨▨

S.–Stile ▨▨▨

SP–Sign post ⌐

✚ –Bridge ⌒

)⦅ View point

ⓣ Telephone ☎

N ↑

1km   1mile

Approximate Scale

71

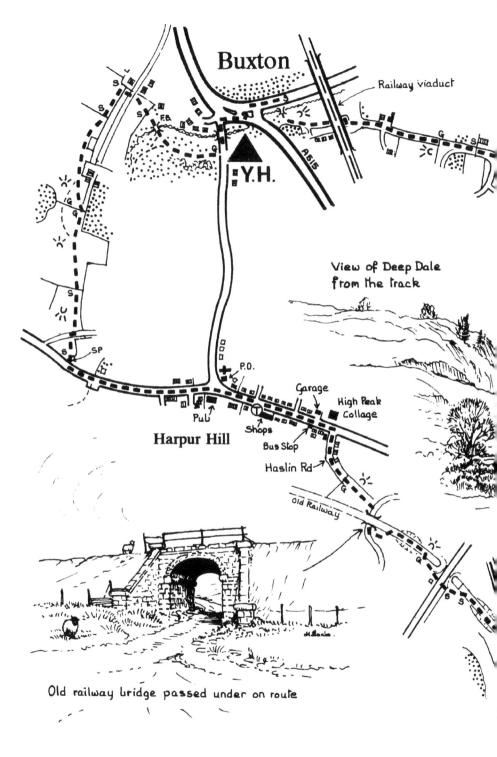

Buxton

Railway viaduct

Y.H.

View of Deep Dale
from the track

P.O.

Garage

High Peak
Collage

Pub

Shops

Bus Stop

Harpur Hill

Haslin Rd

Old Railway

Old railway bridge passed under on route

Map 28
Buxton to Harpur Hill and Deep Dale
see page 45

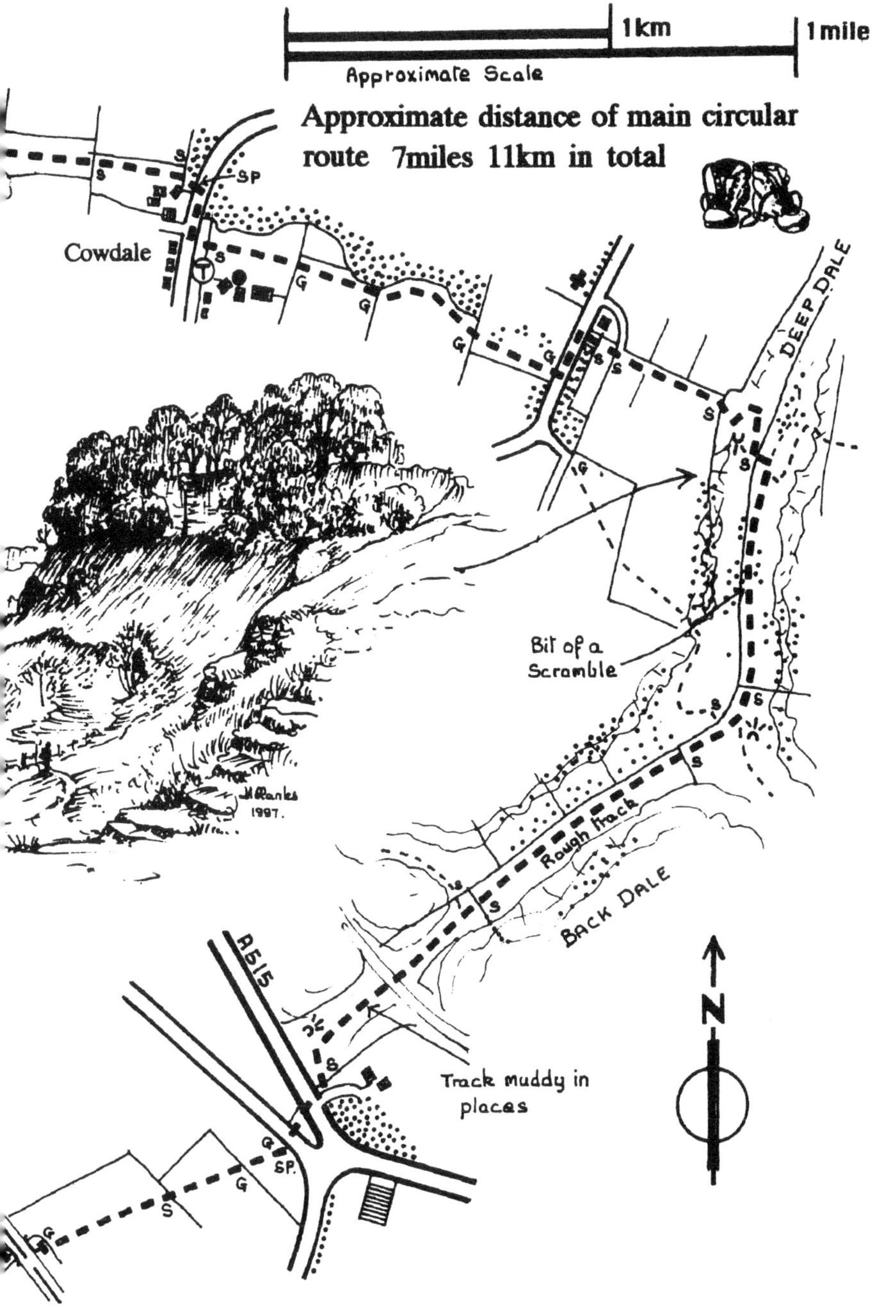

1km | 1 mile

Approximate Scale

Approximate distance of main circular route 7miles 11km in total

Cowdale

DEEP DALE

Bit of a Scramble

M.Ranks 1997.

Rough Track

BACK DALE

A515

Track muddy in places

N

73

Buxton YH to Gradbach Mill YH

Maps 29 / 30 (see pages 78 / 81)

8 miles (12.75km)

This path climbs up onto Axe Edge before descending into the lovely Dane Valley.

From the hostel, proceed over Harpur Hill Road and into the wood opposite. The path skirts the Buxton suburbs before climbing up the valleyside below Grinlow, eventually dropping down to the road between Harpur Hill and the Leek-Buxton road. The path climbs Countess Cliff and heads south to Diamond Hill, named after the clear pieces of quartz found here known as Buxton Diamonds. The route climbs Leap Edge to reach Dalehead and a road, the old coal road from the days of coal mining on Axe Edge to your right.

Turn right and then left on a farm track, heading south to a farm and then bearing right to Brand Top hamlet. Take a look at the War Memorial — this tiny place lost 5 members of one family to the Great War. The path then heads to Dove Head where the River Dove rises (opposite the farm on the county boundary and by the A53 to your right).

Cross the A53 and take the track around Axe Edge End to Drystone Edge where there are several cottages on the lane. Turn left at the T-junction. The right turn leads down to Three Shires Head where Derbyshire meets Staffordshire and Cheshire. At the next T-junction, turn right and follow the track around to Knotbury where a path drops down the fields to Gradbach. There are superb views across the moors to The Roaches on your left.

The path descends into the Dane Valley, a short walk from the youth hostel, housed in an old silk mill.

Buxton YH to Hartington YH

Maps 31 / 32 (see pages 82 / 85)

(OS Outdoor Leisure Map 24)

12 miles (19km)

This is a pleasant walk with a comfortable walkers pub in Crowdecote en-route.

Follow the same route as Buxton YH to Gradbach YH to Dalehead. From here turn left and then right, walking past Thirkelow Farm and heading for Brand End, a steep-sided spur to your right as you approach Booth Farm. The path then cuts across the west flank of Hollins Hill heading for the infant River Dove and the village of Hollinsclough beyond. Look for the little chapel (built in his garden by a packhorse leader or jagger man) and the pretty school, now replaced by a more functional building behind.

Just past the school, a path bears off to the left to reach the River Dove, which is followed to a footbridge. The large hills across the river (Chrome and Parkhouse Hills) are reef limestones — old coral reefs — and are the nearest to peaks in the Peak District, which is named after a tribe, not mountains. From here it is a delightful stroll down the valley through Glutton Bridge to Crowdecote and the Packhorse Inn. Here, our path (a packhorse route, like many paths in this area) crosses another heading from Cheshire into Derbyshire.

Continue down the valley fields to Pilsbury Castle Hill where an interpretation board explains the field evidence. The preferred path then climbs out of the valley to avoid the road which actually sees little traffic. Either way soon brings you into Hartington and a short climb up Hall Bank to the youth hostel.

Walks around Gradbach

(OS Outdoor Leisure Map 24)

Gradbach to Wildboarclough & Three Shires Head

6.5 miles (10.5km)

Maps 33 (see pages 86 / 87)

The area covered by the headwaters of the River Dane and the neighbouring valley of Wildboarclough is both rugged and beautiful; most of it is quiet and the views are extensive. Try it yourself and see if you end the day wondering what made it a little different.

Cross the footbridge by the youth hostel and climb the packhorse road which took silk from the mill to Macclesfield. On reaching the road (another packhorse road heading for Derbyshire via Three Shires Head), the white painted building is an old pub — the Eagle and Child. The inscription above the door, plus a motif on the right wall of the entrance hall showing an eagle and child, are taken from the Arms of Lord Derby who owns Crag Hall at Wildboarclough village.

Continue up the track by the building. As it levels off, Shutlingsloe comes into view ahead beyond Wildboarclough. Cross the A54, skirt the barn and drop down into Wildboarclough Valley. Once over the stile and with the wood on your right, the path may be rather boggy for a short distance. Cross the field and drop down to the Clough Brook, opposite the Crag Inn. Turn right and then right again over the bridge. Climb up the road past the church and hall. Notice the old post office just over the bridge — once the largest subpost office in England. It was part of an old cotton mill built by James Brindley just below the bridge.

At a bend in the road, a track goes left and across the fields and the A54 to Cut Thorn Farm. It is easy to follow to the farm where an unsurfaced track goes down to the Panniers Pool Bridge at Three Shires Head. Cross the old packhorse bridge and take the track to Knotbury before cutting across the fields downhill to return to Gradbach.

Note the short cut on the map. It saves miles but you miss some interesting scenery by taking it.

Gradbach to Wincle   (OS Outdoor Leisure Map 24)

Maps 34 (see pages 88 / 89)   5.5 miles (8.75km)

Take the path by the millhouse to the bridge over the Black Brook. There are a choice of routes from here and all are good. Martyn has chosen the middle one via Lud Church which leaves the landslip to climb the heather-covered moor to reach a ridge path. Turn left, and eventually it drops down to a gate where it joins a holloway. Turn left and follow the track past a farm. Above you on the right is the Hanging Stone with a memorial to a pet dog. The Roaches Estate used to belong to the Brocklehursts of Swythamley Hall, which is now a Transcendental Meditation Centre.

From Hanging Stone Farm a path crosses the fields and drops through a wood to Danebridge. There is a pub here for refreshments but no cafe. Return on the path, starting by the large bridge over the River Dane. It is a very pleasant stroll on a well marked path back to Gradbach above the river meadows, eventually reaching Back Forest for the last mile or so. The path through the wood keeps close to the river but well above it.

Gradbach Mill YH to Meerbrook YH   (OS Outdoor Leisure Map 24)

Map 35 (see pages 90 / 91)   6 miles (9.5km)

The route goes into Back Forest to the impressive landslip known as Lud Church, up onto the heather moor beyond and joins a ridge path with truly spectacular views. The path then climbs up to The Roaches before dropping down to Meerbrook village.

Take the path downstream past the mill house and across the fields to the Black Brook. Cross the footbridge and climb up the wood to Lud Church (not Lud's as on the OS Map). Walk through the huge landslip used by the Luddites (religious dissenters), hence its name. It has nothing to do with the 19th century Luddites. Climb out of the far end onto the moor, and up to the ridge path where you turn left. It is well defined and follows a stone wall to Roach End where you cross the road and climb up onto The Roaches. The path follows the escarpment, past Doxey Pool before dropping down to the road. Look out for Rockhall, a house built into the rock.

From here there is a path that drops directly down to Meerbrook and the cosy little youth hostel. The views are towards Leek, over Tittesworth Reservoir and to the ridge to your right called Gun. From the Roaches you can see over to Morridge to your left, to the high isolated hill called Shutlingsloe to the north and to Bosley Cloud escarpment beyond Gun where the upland meets the Cheshire Plain. Take your camera and hope for clear weather!

Walks around Meerbrook (OS Outdoor Leisure Map 24)

Meerbrook to Turner's Pool & Gun End 5.5 miles (8.75km)
Map 36 (see pages 92 / 93)

Meerbrook is a small village in some good walking country. Although The Roaches are very popular in the summer, most of these paths are much quieter.

Turn right beyond the church on a path that runs in a virtual straight line up the lower flank of Gun Hill, with good views to your right up to The Roaches. Just beyond Meadows Farm, the path bears to the left to pass Hazelwood House and reach Turner's Pool, a large and picturesque pool used by fishermen.

The path now climbs gently uphill to Gun End for refreshments at the tea room. If it is a nice day, tea and cakes in the garden is recommended. You have to retrace your steps about 3/4 mile to regain the path to Meerbrook. This is fairly flat to Old Hay Top Farm, before dropping down to Lower Wetwood and then across the fields to Meerbrook.

Meerbrook to Upper Hulme and The Roaches

Map 37 (see pages 94 / 95) 8.5 miles (13km)

Take the road across Tittesworth Reservoir and turn left for Upper Hulme at Middle Hulme Farm. This is an old saltway into the Peak and is used in the **Walks around Hartington**. It is the path from Sheen to Hartington. The path soon reaches Upper Hulme which grew when a dye house, now closed, was built here. There is a pub in the village, the only one on this walk. The only cafe is on the road to The Roaches from Upper Hulme (see map).

Note the alternative path from Upper Hulme to the Blue Hills area between The Roaches and Ramshaw Rocks (off the top of the map). The path swings westwards to climb up onto The Roaches and return on the path mentioned on the Gradbach YH - Meerbrook YH walk.

Walk around Tittesworth Reservoir 5.5 miles (9km)

This reservoir, built as a compensating source of water for the dyers in Leek who took so much out of the River Churnet, was extended considerably nearly 40 years ago. There is a walk around it which takes about 2.5 hours. There is a good visitor centre, cafe and children's play area the Meerbrook end just over the bridge at the end of the village. Photographers often try their luck from the bridge — if conditions are right you can get a lovely reflection of The Roaches in the water.

Martyn has a list of 57 different birds sighted around or on the reservoir by a YHA member, so good spotting!

Walks around Dimmingsdale

(OS Pathfinder Map 810)

Dimmingsdale to Croxden Abbey

9 miles (14.5km)

Map 38 (see pages 96 / 97)

A walk to the imposing remains of the Cistercian Abbey southwest of Alton.

Descend down into Dimmingsdale and turn right to walk up the valley with the pools on your left. Pass the unusual circular house. Continue on to reach the lane at Greendale. Turn left here to climb out of the valley to the A5032 — the Alton to Cheadle road — near to Threapwood.

The path cuts across the fields heading towards Greatgate, the 'gate' or entrance to the former abbey. The map shows a diversion to The Raddle, a nearby pub, before continuing on to the abbey remains. The village road cuts across the site of the altar, but the remains are still substantial, especially at the west end of the church. These are now in the care of English Heritage.

Return from Greatgate to Dimmingsdale via Bradley in the Moors, descending down the wood from Alton Common to reach the pools below the youth hostel.

Note: if time permits, upon reaching Greendale continue up the road until you reach the entrance to the large Hawksmoor Nature Reserve, owned by the National Trust. It is basically a large wooded area, descending down into the Churnet Valley.

A three miles (4.75km) walk around Dimmingsdale is also shown on the map.

Exploring the Churnet Valley: 1

Dimmingsdale to Oakamoor

Map 39 (see pages 98 / 99)

3 miles (4.75km)

Two short circular routes around the lovely Churnet Valley. Take the path which drops steeply down through the wood to join the valley road. Turn left and walk up the road to Oakamoor. You pass a country park made on the site of an old copper works. The first transatlantic cable was made here in 1856. Cross the bridge with the big millpool on the upstream-side. At the end of the bridge you can see marked on the wall where the old canal passed under the road until 1846. It ran from Froghall to Uttoxeter, with the former valley railway running down much of its course. A path at the end of the bridge starts on the right and follows the river to join the old railway track. Follow this down to Lord's Bridge. Cross the river to the cafe and either return directly to the youth hostel or walk up Dimmingsdale and then turn right uphill. This walk may be extended by continuing with the next walk in reverse.

Exploring the Churnet Valley: 2 (see page 100)

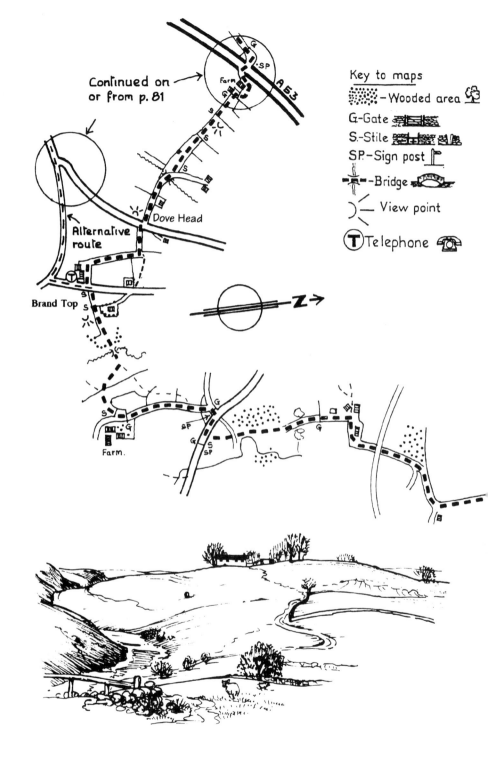

Continued on or from p. 81

A53

Farm

Alternative route

Dove Head

Brand Top

Farm.

Z →

Key to maps

⬚ – Wooded area 🌳

G – Gate

S. – Stile

SP – Sign post

✚ – Bridge

)⚊ – View point

T Telephone ☎

Map 29
Buxton YH to Gradbach Mill YH: 1
see page 74

Approximate distance of main
route 8miles 12.75km

Buxton Youth Hostel
Tel- 01298-22287

1km
1mile
Approximate Scale

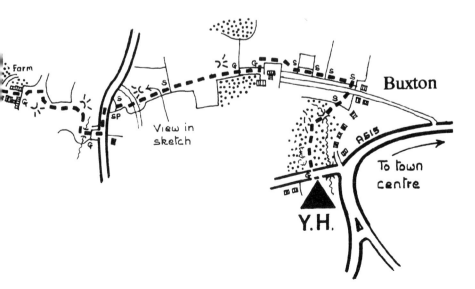

Farm

View in
sketch

Buxton

A515

To town
centre

Y.H.

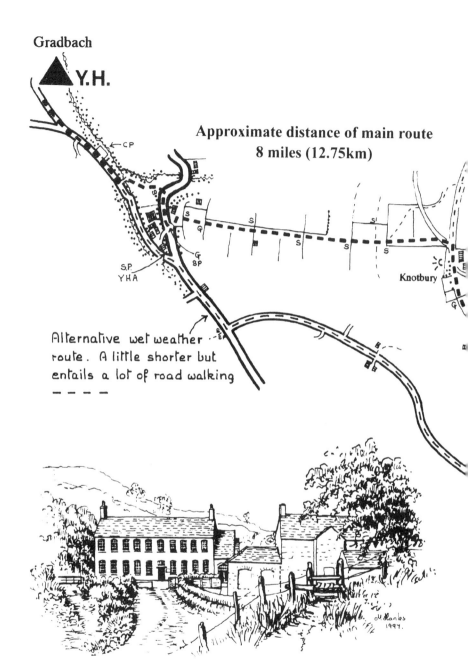

Gradbach

Y.H.

**Approximate distance of main route
8 miles (12.75km)**

Knotbury

Alternative wet weather
route. A little shorter but
entails a lot of road walking
— — — —

Gradbach Mill Youth Hostel
Tel: 01260-227625

Map 30
Buxton YH to Gradbach Mill YH: 2
see page 74

View from the track

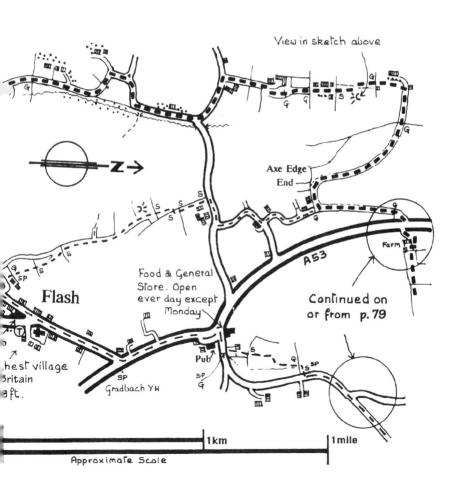

View in sketch above

Axe Edge End

Farm

A53

Food & General Store. Open ever day except Monday

Continued on or from p. 79

Flash

Pub

hest village Britain aft.

SP
Gradbach YH

1km   1mile

Approximate Scale

Map 31
Buxton YH to Hartington YH: 1
see page 74

Approximate distance 12 miles 19 km

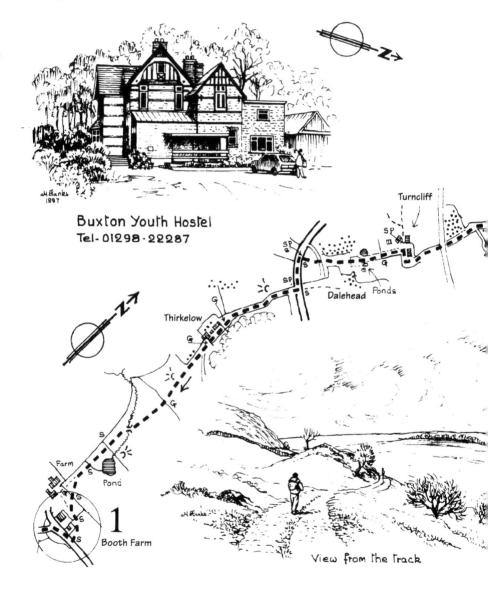

Buxton Youth Hostel
Tel- 01298-22287

Turncliff

Thirkelow

Dalehead   Ponds

Farm

Pond

1
Booth Farm

View from the track

It is recommended that an O.S. map is also used when making this walk

Town Centre

BUXTON

A515

Y.H.

1

Hollinsclough

Farm

CG
Barn

SP

2

CG

The attractive village of Hollinsclough

1km   1mile

Approximate Scale

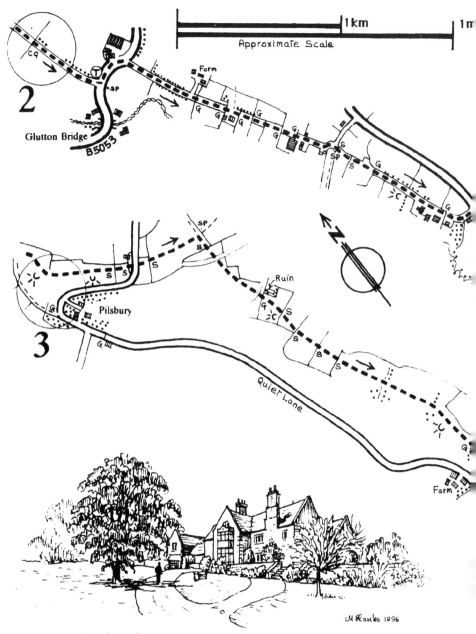

2

CG

1km   1m

Approximate Scale

Farm

SP

G   G   G   G

G   G

G   G

S

SP   S   G

C

G

Glutton Bridge

B5053

3

SP

S

S

C

S   S   S

Ruin

G   C   S

G

Pilsbury

S

G

S

Quiet Lane

C

G

Farm

M.Hawkes 1996

Hartington Hall Youth Hostel
Tel- 01298-84223

Map 32
Buxton YH to Hartington YH: 2
see page 74

& od Crowdecote

Crowdecote

It is recommended the OS
White Peak area map 2½ to 1 mile
is also used when walking this route

Pilsbury
Castle Hill

3

HARTINGTON

Y.H.

Lane along the route

85

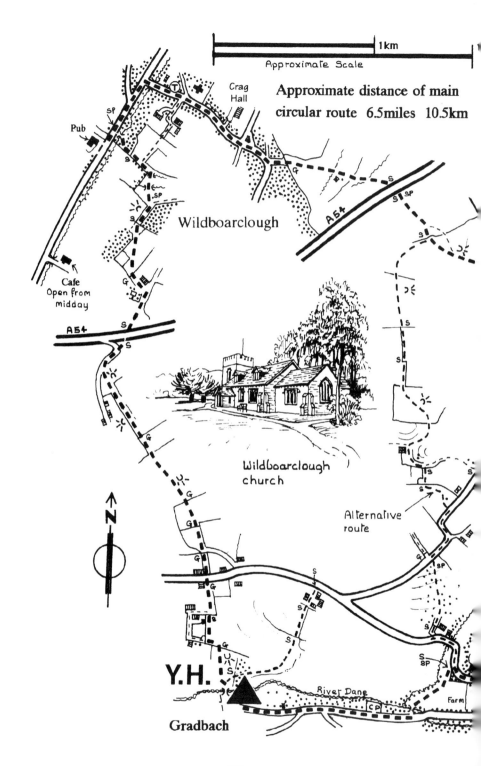

1km
Approximate Scale

Crag
Hall

Approximate distance of main
circular route 6.5miles 10.5km

Pub

SP

Wildboarclough

A54

Cafe
Open from
midday

A54

N

Wildboarclough
church

Alternative
route

Y.H.

River Dane

Farm

CP

Gradbach

86

Map 33
Gradbach to Wildboarclough and Three Shires Head
see page 74

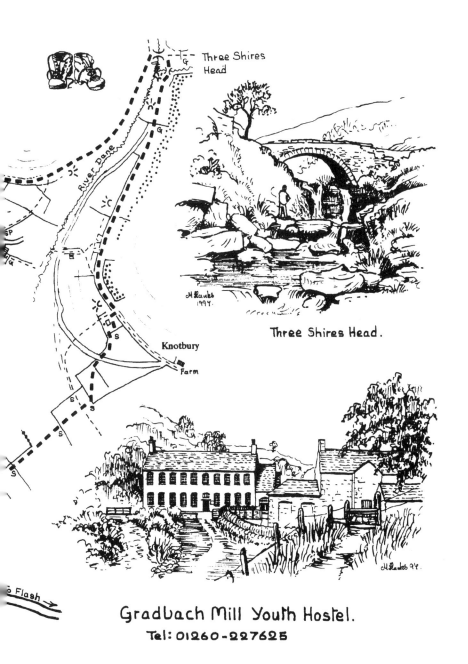

Three Shires Head.

Gradbach Mill Youth Hostel.
Tel: 01260-227625

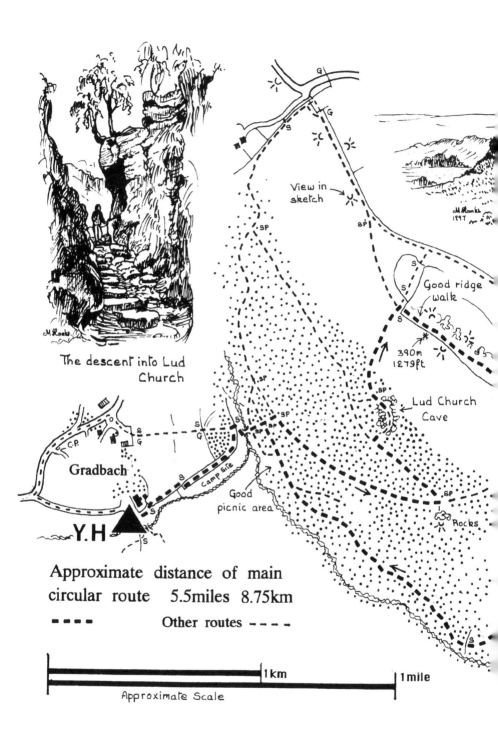

The descent into Lud Church

View in sketch

Good ridge walk

390m 1279ft

Lud Church Cave

Gradbach

C.P.

Camp Site

Good picnic area

Rocks

Y.H

Approximate distance of main circular route   5.5miles 8.75km

▬ ▬ ▬ ▬   Other routes ‐ ‐ ‐ ‐

1km   1mile

Approximate Scale

M Ranks 1897

Map 34
Gradbach to Wincle
see page 75

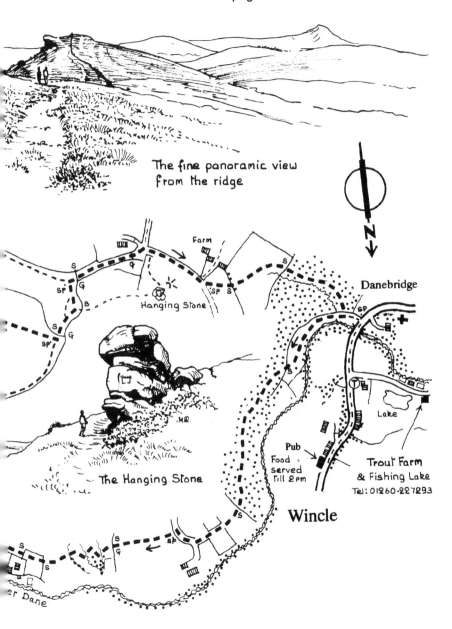

The fine panoramic view
from the ridge

Farm

Hanging Stone

Danebridge

The Hanging Stone

Lake

Pub
Food
served
Till 2pm

Trout Farm
& Fishing Lake
Tel: 01260-227293

Wincle

er Dane

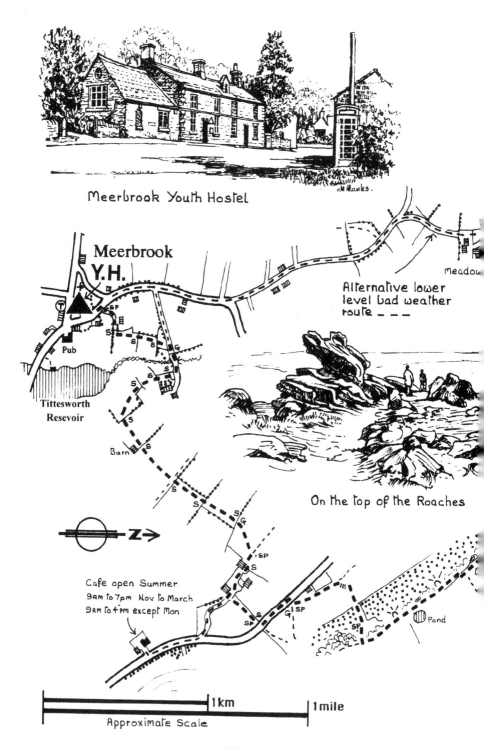

Meerbrook Youth Hostel

Meerbrook
Y.H.

Alternative lower
level bad weather
route _ _ _

meadow

Pub

Tittesworth
Resevoir

Barn

On the top of the Roaches

Z→

Cafe open Summer
9am to 7pm Nov to March
9am to 4pm except Mon

SP

S

SP S

G SP

SP

Pond

1km   1mile

Approximate Scale

Map 35
Gradbach Mill YH to Meerbrook YH
see page 75

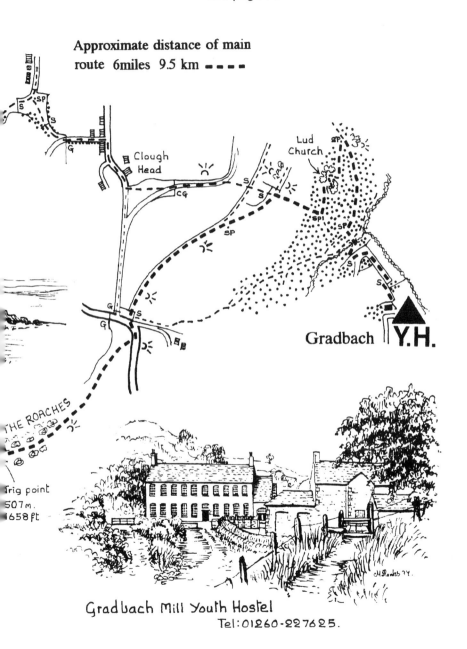

Approximate distance of main
route 6miles 9.5 km ▬ ▬ ▬

Lud
Church

Clough
Head

Gradbach Y.H.

THE ROACHES

Trig point
507m.
1658ft

Gradbach Mill Youth Hostel
Tel: 01260-227625.

91

Map 36
Meerbrook to Turner's Pool and Gun End
see page 76

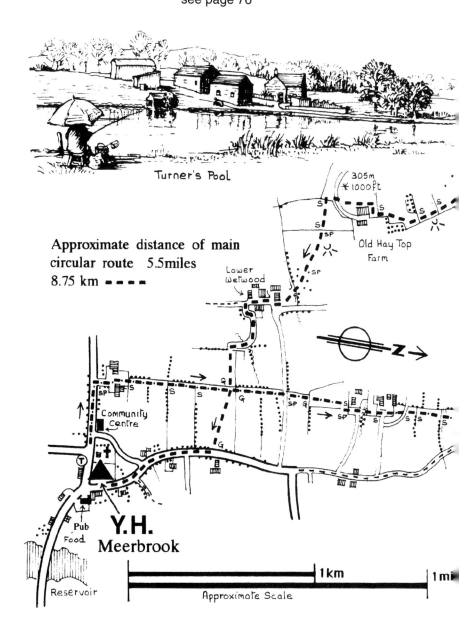

Turner's Pool

305m
*1000ft

Approximate distance of main
circular route   5.5miles
8.75 km ▬ ▬ ▬ ▬

Old Hay Top
Farm

Lower
Wetwood

Community
Centre

Y.H.
Pub
Food
Meerbrook

Reservoir

1km   1mi

Approximate Scale

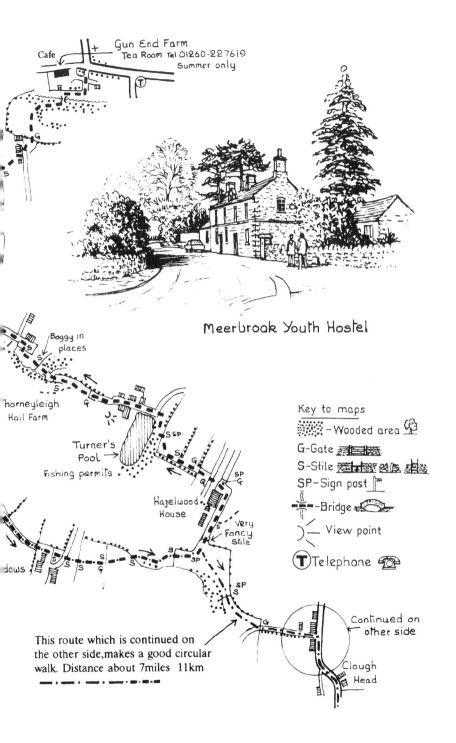

Gun End Farm
Tea Room Tel 01260-227619
Summer only

Cafe

Meerbrook Youth Hostel

Boggy in places

Thorneyleigh Hall Farm

Turner's Pool →
Fishing permits

Hazelwood House

Very Fancy Stile

dows

Key to maps

▨ – Wooded area 🌳
G – Gate
S – Stile
SP – Sign post
–‖– – Bridge
)⏜– View point
Ⓣ Telephone ☎

Continued on other side

Clough Head

This route which is continued on the other side, makes a good circular walk. Distance about 7 miles 11km

93

Map 37
Meerbrook to Upper Hulme and The Roaches
see page 76

The Blue F

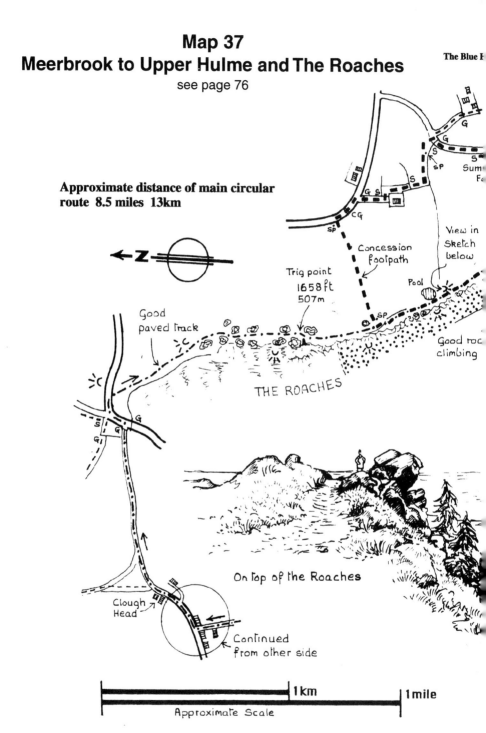

Approximate distance of main circular route 8.5 miles 13km

←Z

Concession footpath

Trig point
1658 ft
507m

View in Sketch below

Pool

Good paved track

Good roc climbing

THE ROACHES

On Top of the Roaches

Clough Head

Continued from other side

1km   1mile

Approximate Scale

94

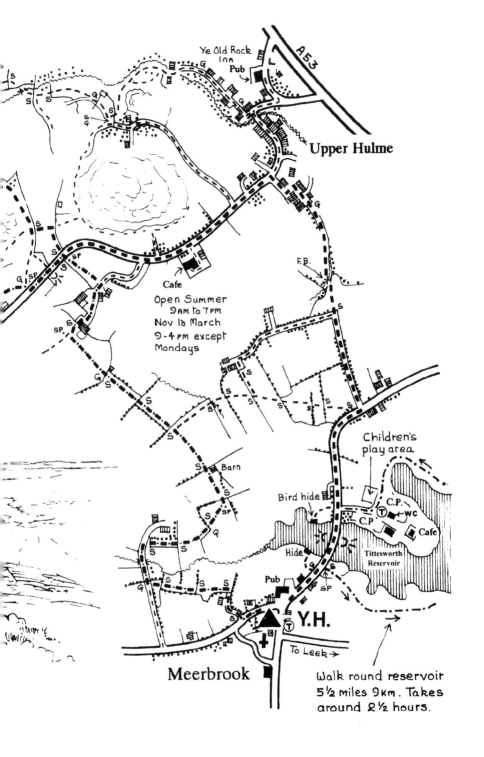

Ye Old Rock Inn
Pub

A53

Upper Hulme

Cafe

Open Summer
9am to 7pm
Nov to March
9-4 pm except
Mondays

F.B.

Children's
play area

Barn

Bird hide

C.P.
wc
C.P

Cafe

Hide

Tittesworth
Reservoir

Pub

Y.H.

To Leek →

Meerbrook

Walk round reservoir
5½ miles 9km. Takes
around 2½ hours.

M.Panks
1997

Dimmingsdale Youth Hostel
Tel: 01538-702304

Approximate distance of mai
circular route   9miles 14.5 km
- - -
Other route
3miles   4.75 km ━o━o

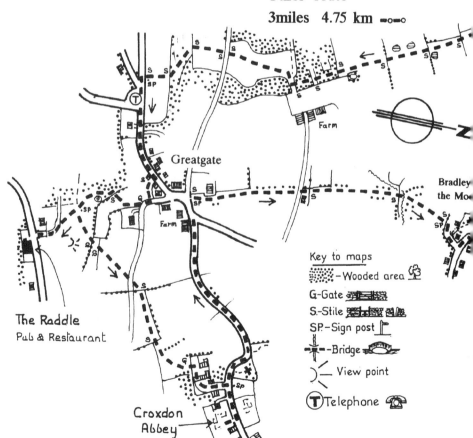

Greatgate

Farm

Bradley
the Mo

Farm

The Raddle
Pub & Restaurant

Croxdon
Abbey

Key to maps
▒▒▒ –Wooded area 🌳
G-Gate ▨▤▥
S.-Stile ▨▤▥
S.P.–Sign post 🚩
━╬━–Bridge 🌉
)–(View point
Ⓣ Telephone ☎

Map 38
Dimmingsdale to Croxden Abbey
see page 77

Croxdon Abbey

Now a well preserved ruin

Approximate Scale

1km   1mile

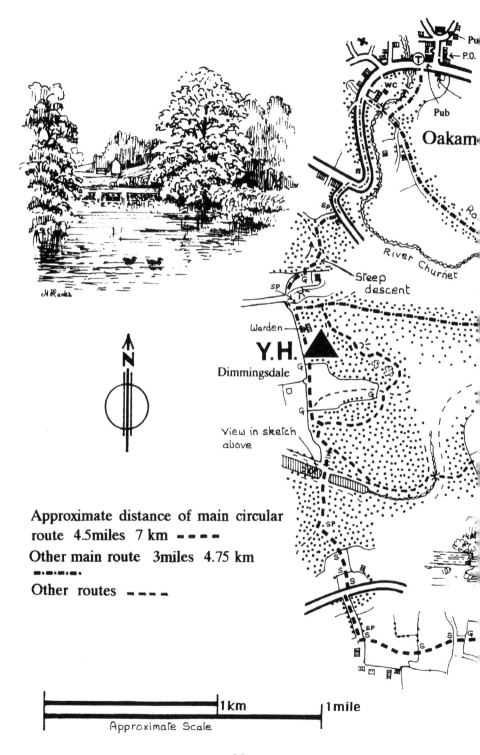

Approximate distance of main circular
route 4.5miles 7 km ----
Other main route 3miles 4.75 km
-.-.-.-.
Other routes ----

1km

1mile

Approximate Scale

98

Map 39
Exploring the Churnet Valley
see page 77

Alton Castle

Lord,s Bridge

SP

Cafe   C.P.

Alton Towers
Theme Park

View in
sketch
above

SP

Castle
Not open to
the public

Pub

SP

Pub

Pub

Pub

P.O. Shop

Ramblers Retreat Cafe at
Lords Bridge

Pub

General
Store. Food

Alton

Exploring the Churnet Valley: 2

Dimmingsdale to Alton   **(OS Pathfinder Map 810)**
Map 39 (see pages 98 / 99)   4.5 miles (7km)

Cross Dimmingsdale and climb out of the far side of the valley. Cross the B5032 to a lane before turning left to follow the fields to Alton. The path has views across the valley to Alton Towers.

Alton is a lovely village with six pubs! Look out for the old lock-up opposite the general store. The Norman Castle remains are minimal and the current building, looking like a Rhineland castle from the valley, was designed by Pugin in the 1840s. It's now a prep school. The mill by the ornate river bridge is an old copper slitting mill. Here Guinea rods were made for use as currency in Africa as part of the slave trade. The former station building opposite has been preserved by the Landmark Trust. Return to Lord's Bridge up the old railway track and then use one of the two paths mentioned in the path to Oakamoor.

If you are staying at Dimmingsdale and walking to Alton Towers, proceed directly to the Rambler's Retreat cafe, cross Lord's Bridge and climb up through the road to reach the road by the Pink Lodge. Turn left and walk about 800 yards (700m) to reach the park entrance. In addition to the theme park and the hell-fire rides that test your nerve and G-force resistance, the large Tudor Gothic house can be explored externally or at roof level and the huge and lovely garden — occupying a whole valley — can also be visited. The garden is at its best at the end of May/early June. There is no reduction for visitors wishing to see only the garden.

This walk may be extended by continuing with the previous walk in reverse.
Exploring the Churnet Valley: 1 (see page 77)

Dimmingsdale YH to Ilam Hall YH   (OS Outdoor Leisure Map 24 and OS Pathfinder Map 810)

Maps 40 / 41 (see pages 104 / 107)   11 miles (17km)

The path drops down through the wood to Dimmingsdale, which has a series of lakes impounded for an old lead smelter, now a house. The valley is particularly beautiful in the autumn. The path reaches the valley road by the Rambler's Retreat Cafe. Cross the road and follow the track over the River Churnet to the old railway line. Join this and walk past Alton Station. The building by the bridge over the river was once a brass wire mill dating from 1739, although the building is even older.

After about another mile, take a path to the left, over the old canal (abandoned in 1846) and head for another valley with a series of relatively new and beautiful lakes. Much of the land here is part of the Bamford family estate (the JCB excavators are made in nearby Rocester). By the second lake, the path meets a minor road. Turn right and look for a gap in the high stonewall on your left. The path now passes through the deer park to Wootton Lodge, one of the finest country houses in Staffordshire.

By the lodge, turn left and head for Wootton and then by a series of fields, head for Stanton there is no pub in either of these villages). Just past Stanton post office turn left, heading for Swinscoe, which is reached after crossing Cuckoo Cliff Dell. Note the deviation from the path to the pub (Dog & Partridge). Cross the A52 along a green lane before descending down the fields to Blore. If it is open, the church here is worth a visit for its alabaster monuments to the Bassett family. However the path passes to the west of the hamlet and a short detour along the road is necessary, rejoining the path at the car park at Blore Pastures, shown on the map.

From here, the path descends into the Manifold Valley and reaches Wood Lodge by the River Manifold. It is a short but pleasant stroll from here alongside the river to St Bertram's Bridge where you can see Ilam Hall above.

Note: The Pathfinder map is to be replaced by a new Explorer map.

Walks around Ilam (OS Outdoor Leisure Map 24)

Ilam to Throwley, Wetton and Castern
Map 42 (see pages 108 / 109) 8.75 miles (14 km)

From Ilam Hall, walk down to the river and turn upstream. Look for the boil holes where first the River Manifold and then the River Hamps boil up to the surface, having travelled underground from Wetton Mill and Waterhouses respectively.

The path known as Paradise Walk fully justifies its name. Cross the river and then go across the fields to Musden where you join a little-used road to Throwley Hall. There are good views across the Manifold Valley from this road. The ruined old hall may be seen. From Throwley, head for the trees on the skyline before descending to Beeston Tor Farm, where the Hamps Valley reaches the Manifold Valley. The path leaves the farm at Throwley by a circular tank and then goes through a little copse to reach a large field. The farm has a bull which sometimes is loose in this field. Given a wide berth, there should be no problems.

Having reached the Manifold Valley, follow the roadway to Weags Bridge with the old Manifold railway track on your left. Cross the bridge and climb out of the valley. Bear left to Wetton and cross the fields to reach the village. The Royal Oak pub serves food until 2pm.

Return through the fields bounded by stone walls to reach the Manifold Valley. The path runs across the top of the valley with magnificent views. The valley side is a nature reserve at this point. There are mineshafts in the area, which should be avoided. The path eventually leaves the valley edge and heads to Castern Hall, where you descend back into the valley to Ilam.

For a short circular route of 2.5 miles (4km), take the route to Musden Farm and then walk down to the river and Rushley Bridge. Continue around to River Lodge and return to Ilam down the side of the river. At the Lodge, look at the inscription above the door. It refers to Jemima, Countess of Monteglass. She was the oldest daughter of Jessie Watts-Russell who built the current Ilam Hall.

Ilam to Stanhope, Mill Dale and Dovedale 8.5 miles (13.5km)
Map 43 (see pages 110 / 111)

A walk over Ilam Tops to the dry valley known as Hall Dale and then on to Mill Dale for refreshments before returning down Dovedale to Ilam.

Walk through the village and a short distance on the road to Thorpe, before turning left. A path climbs straight up the hill called Bunster in front of you, but your path is the more gradual climb to the left! Pass the pond and climb up the fields. Look out for the ancient terraces (called strip lynchets) which you pass en-route as you climb up towards Ilam Tops Farm.

Here the path turns right for Air Cottage which is situated over looking the valley of Dovedale. Continue along the edge of the valley top before descending down to the riverside path in Dovedale. Upon leaving the wood, turn left and walk up Hall Dale to Stanshope, Turn left across a couple of fields to reach the old way to Mill Dale. Descend to the latter where there is a tea-bar and toilets.

Cross the packhorse bridge (Viator's Bridge). It is named from a dialogue between Izaak Walton and Charles Cotton about the bridge in Walton's Complete Angler (6th edition). Look back at the bridge; you can see that the walls were added later. Packhorse bridges had low side walls to avoid interfering with the panniers.

From here there is a delightful stroll down Dovedale to Ilam. Look out for the tors and outcrops, the crystal clear water and the ancient ash wood. The whole area is now a National nature reserve. Below Thorpe Cloud, you can cross via the stepping stones (but not when the river is high) or carry on to the footbridge by the car park.

From here, a path heads for the rear of the Izaac Walton Hotel and then on to Ilam.

Ilam YH to Hartington YH

Maps 44 / 45 (see pages 112 / 115)

(OS Outdoor Leisure Map 24)

8.5 miles (13.5km)

Although this route is lovely whichever way it is walked, walking upstream gives you a better view of the weirs on the river. It has the disadvantage that the sun is behind you, so it's your choice!

From the cross in Ilam village, walk past the last few houses to the stile. A path crosses the fields and passes the rear of the Izaak Walton Hotel before dropping down to the River Dove by the car park. Cross the river by the footbridge and proceed up the east side of the river (unless the river is in flood, you can continue up the road and instead use the stepping stones).

The path follows the river up Dovedale to Mill Dale. The whole route is a nature reserve (SSS1 Grade 1) through a limestone valley (or dale) clothed with relict ashwoods and lots of limestone tors. A small shop at Mill Dale sells tea over the counter onto the street. The main path continues up the valley. If you want the pub, take the alternative green lane up and out of the valley to Alstonefield. The George Inn is a popular ramblers' pub.

The main route follows the road through Mill Dale, past numerous weirs to Lode Mill where the disused corn mill remains. It was a lead smelting mill, hence the name. From here, a path by the bridge (on the Derbyshire bank) follows the river through Wolfscote Dale and Beresford Dale before leaving the river to cross fields to reach Hartington. Notice the difference in the valley compared to Dovedale — it's less wooded and there are few tors. Beresford Dale used to be well-wooded until it was decimated by Dutch Elm desease.

This is a very popular route and much of it has a crushed limestone base to the footpath. However, if you are starting after breakfast, the position of Ilam YH and Hartington YH means that you have a head start on most visitors and you will have a couple of hours of comparative solitude.

Walks around Hartington

(OS Outdoor Leisure Map 24)

This area has some superb circular walks and here are two of them, offering the opportunity to walk across the limestone plateau and alongside the River Dove.

Hartington to Pilsbury & Sheen

Map 46 (see pages 116 / 117)

6 miles (9.5km)

Walk down Hall Bank, cross the road and climb up Hide Lane, with the church on your right. By the new farm house, take the stile and follow the path along the top of the valley to Pilsbury where the path drops down to the hamlet in the valley. A detour to the early Norman wooden-built castle may be made. An interpretation board explains the layout.

From Pilsbury, cross the footbridge over the River Dove. Centuries ago, this old packhorse route was a major saltway into the Peak. Bear left to climb out of the valley to reach the Sheen-Longnor ridge road. A path leads back to Hartington from Harris Close Farm. An alternative route is to continue down the lane into Sheen where there is a pub (The Staffordshire Knot).

A path from Sheen (another packhorse way) leads back to Hartington through a small cutting (called Watergap) before dropping down to a footbridge. If you are staying in the village all day, this bridge is ideal for a picnic lunch. From here, it is a short walk through the river meadows to reach the village by Hartington Cheese Factory.

102

The road from Hartington to Pilsbury is usually quiet, though flat walking on a hard surface. It passes Pool Hall (next to Moat Hall) which was a youth hostel in the 1930s.

Hartington, Biggin Dale & Wolfscote Dale
Map 47 (see pages 118 / 119)   6 miles
(9.5km)

Take the lane opposite the youth hostel and follow it to Biggin Dale. Part of it crosses open fields before reaching an adjacent lane. Upon reaching the dry valley known as Biggin Dale, turn right and follow it down to Wolfscote Dale and the River Dove. If you wish to return to Hartington turn right here. Alternatively, if you wish to go an extra 3 miles to take in Alstonefield village, bear left. Ignore the stepping stones and continue on to a footbridge. It is a steep climb out of the valley to join an unmetalled lane across the fields to the village. There is a good ramblers' pub here — The George. Return on an alternative path to the River Dove and the stepping stones.

Walk up-river back to Hartington. The valley is one of the prettiest in Derbyshire. Wolfscote Dale is left behind as one crosses a field to reach Beresford Dale. Here there is a footbridge and stepping stones adjacent to the old ford. Continue up-river through the short but lovely Beresford Dale. Look back to try and see Beresford Tower, a prospect tower to the demolished Beresford Hall. Also, as one leaves the wooded dale, look through the trees to see the Fishing Temple, built in 1674 by Izaak Walton and Charles Cotton.

After leaving the trees (many of which were lost to Dutch Elm Disease) the path crosses several fields to reach the village by Rookes's Pottery.

Hartington YH to Youlgreave YH
Maps 48 / 49 (see pages 120 / 123)   9 miles (14km)

This path crosses the limestone plateau of the White Peak before following the upper reaches of Bradford Dale. The latter has a clear stream which is impounded near to Youlgreave to create a group of attractive pools.

Take the path to Old Lane just above the hostel and follow the lane for a short distance before heading east through Heathcote to reach the Tissington Trail at the former Hartington Station. The signal box here has been preserved as an information centre and there are photos of the former railway. From the B5054, bear left on a green lane to reach the High Peak Trail (the former Cromford & High Peak Railway of 1828), and turn right to reach Friden Brick Works. This produces silica bricks from local sand deposits in the limestone.

Walk along the B5056 to reach Long Dale. Turn right into the shallow Long Dale; after a short distance, the dale is crossed by an ancient track called the Peak Way. This is followed towards Middleton before turning right to reach the upper reaches of the stream which runs to Bradford Dale. Unfortunately, the latter is a short valley and this route leaves it part way along its length, albeit after the prettiest section. Youlgreave spills down to the river at one point, indicating your arrival. There is a cafe and pubs in the village, but nowhere to eat en-route from Hartington.

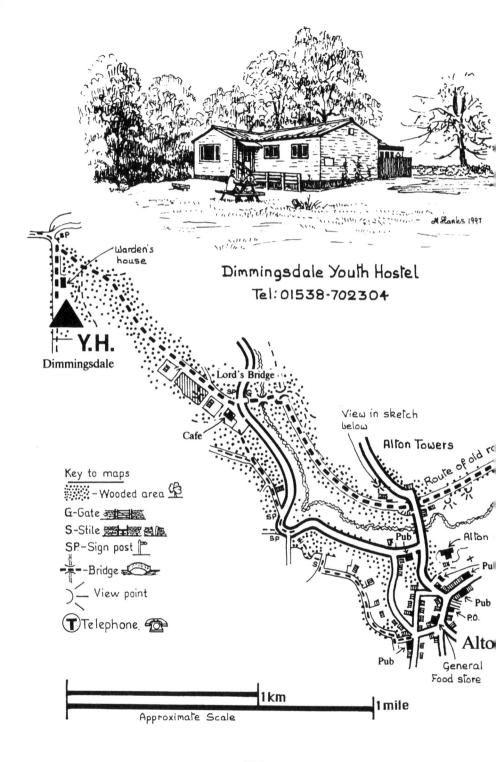

Dimmingsdale Youth Hostel
Tel: 01538-702304

Warden's house

Y.H.
Dimmingsdale

Lord's Bridge

Cafe

View in sketch below

Alton Towers

Route of old ro

Key to maps

▦ —Wooded area 🌳
G-Gate ▦
S.-Stile ▦
SP.-Sign post ⌐
—Bridge ⌒
View point
ⓉTelephone. ☎

Pub

Alton

Alton

Pu

Pub

P.O.

Alto

Pub

General Food store

1km

1 mile

Approximate Scale

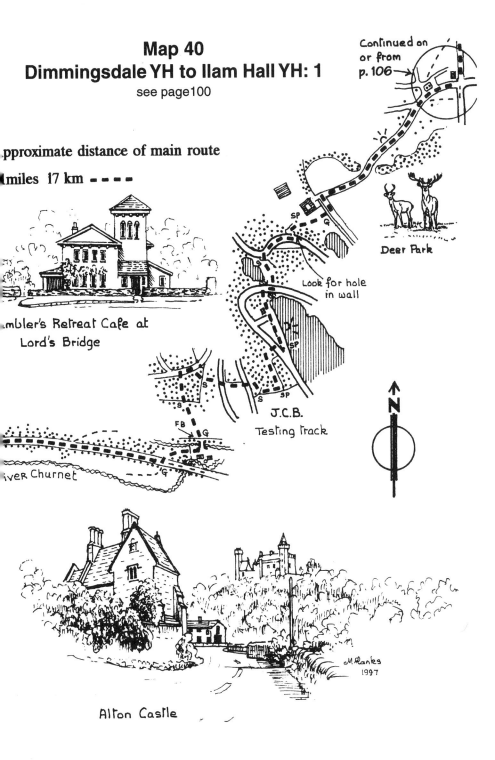

Map 40
Dimmingsdale YH to Ilam Hall YH: 1
see page 100

Continued on or from p. 106 →

pproximate distance of main route

miles 17 km - - - -

Deer Park

.mbler's Retreat Cafe at
Lord's Bridge

Look for hole in wall

N

J.C.B.
Testing Track

iver Churnet

Alton Castle

M. Banks
1997

105

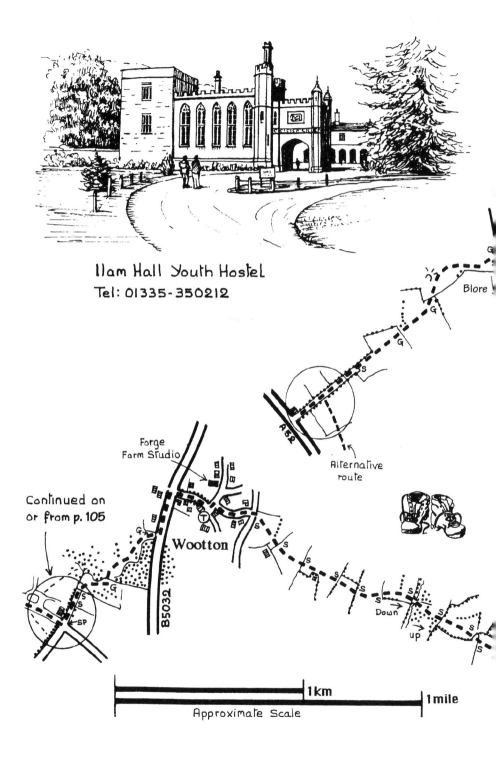

Ilam Hall Youth Hostel
Tel: 01335-350212

Blore

A52

Alternative route

Forge Farm Studio

Continued on or from p. 105

Wootton

B5032

Down

up

1km

1mile

Approximate Scale

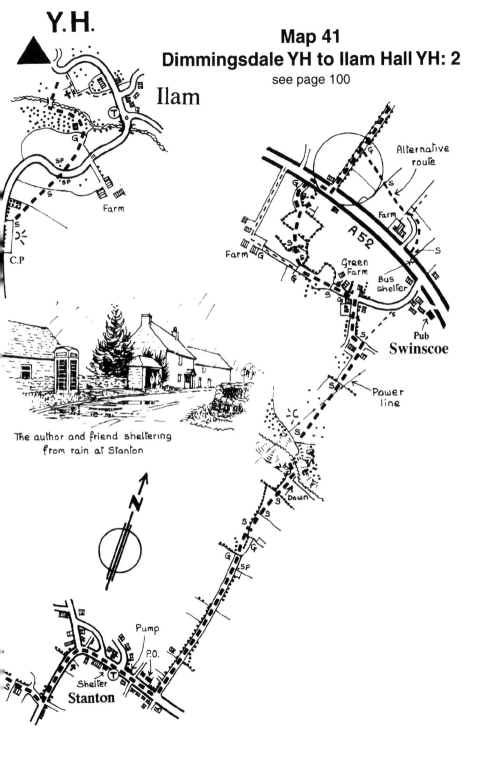

Map 41
Dimmingsdale YH to Ilam Hall YH: 2
see page 100

Y.H.

Ilam

Farm

C.P

Alternative route

Farm

A 52

Green Farm

Bus shelter

Farm

Pub

Swinscoe

Power line

Dawn

The author and friend sheltering from rain at Stanton

N

Pump

P.O.

Shelter

Stanton

107

Map 42
Ilam to Throwley, Wetton and Castern
see page 101

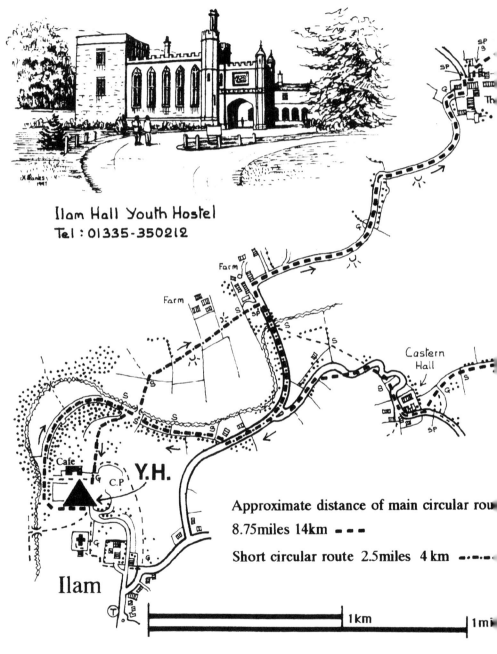

Ilam Hall Youth Hostel
Tel : 01335-350212

Farm

Farm

Castern
Hall

Cafe

Y.H.

C.P

Ilam

Approximate distance of main circular rou

8.75miles 14km - - -

Short circular route 2.5miles 4 km -.-.-

1km

1 mi

108

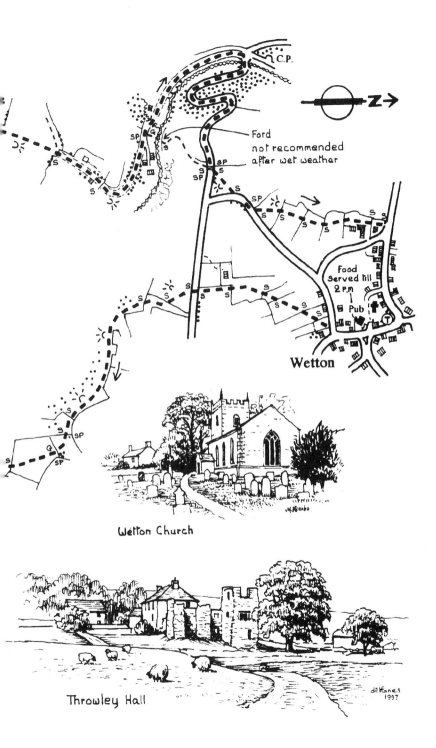

C.P.

Ford
not recommended
after wet weather

Food
Served till
2 p.m.

Pub

Wetton

Wetton Church

Throwley Hall

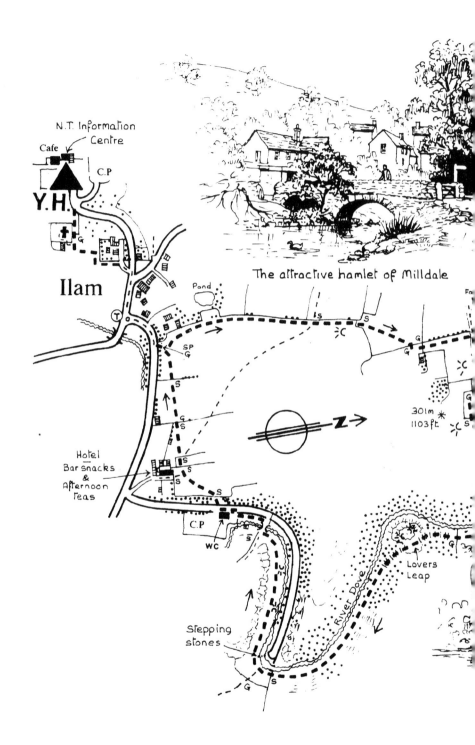

N.T. Information Centre

Cafe

C.P

Y.H.

Ilam

The attractive hamlet of Milldale

Pond

SP
G

Hotel
Bar snacks
&
Afternoon
Teas

C.P

WC

Stepping
stones

Lovers
Leap

River Dove

301m
1103ft

Map 43
Ilam to Stanhope, Mill Dale and Dovedale

see page 101

1km | 1mile

Approximate Scale

Approximate distance of main circular route
8.5miles 13.5km
Circular route to Ilam Rock 5.5miles 9 km

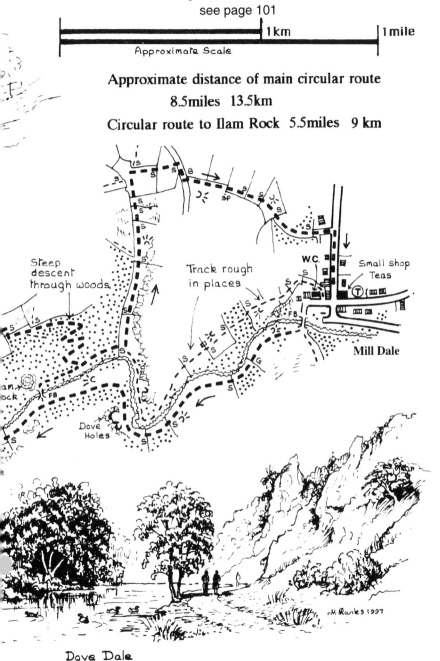

Steep
descent
through woods

Track rough
in places

W.C.

Small shop
Teas

Mill Dale

Dove
Holes

Ilam
Rock

FB

Dove Dale

Map 44
Ilam YH to Hartington YH: 1
see page 102

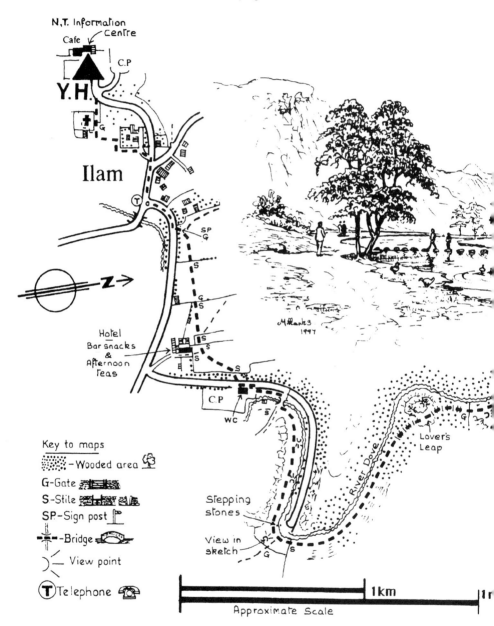

N.T. Information Centre
Cafe
C.P
Y.H.
G
Ilam
T
SP G
S
-Z→
G
S
Hotel Bar snacks & Afternoon Teas
S
S
S
S
C.P
WC
River Dove
Lover's Leap
G
Stepping stones
View in sketch
G
S

Key to maps
⣿⣿⣿ –Wooded area
G–Gate
S–Stile
SP–Sign post
–Bridge
View point
T Telephone

1km
1r
Approximate Scale

Millantes 1997

Ilam Hall Youth Hostel
Tel: 01335-350212

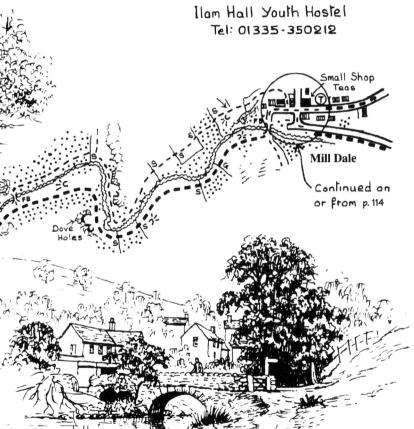

Small Shop
Teas

Mill Dale

Continued on or from p. 114

Dove Holes

The attractive hamlet of mill Dale

Map 45
Ilam YH to Hartington YH: 2

see page 102

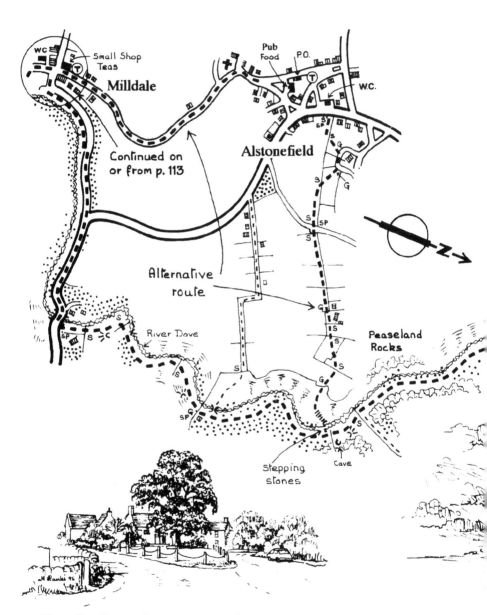

WC

Small Shop
Teas

Milldale

Pub
Food

P.O.

W.C.

Continued on
or from p. 113

Alstonefield

Alternative
route

River Dove

Peaseland
Rocks

Stepping
stones

Cave

The attractive village of Alstonefield

114

Approximate distance by either routes

8.5miles 13.5 km. ----

Hartington Hall Youth Hostel
Tel - 01298-84223

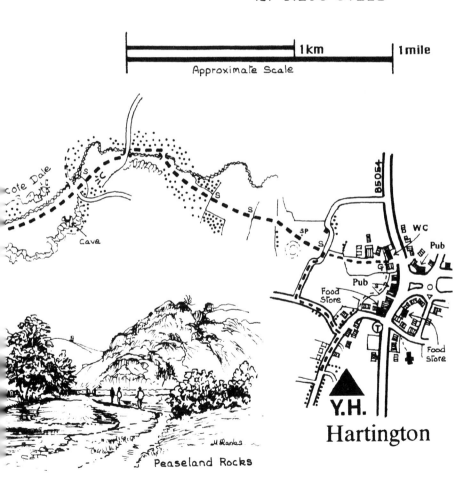

Peaseland Rocks

Y.H.
Hartington

Map 46
Hartington to Pilsbury and Sheen
see page 102

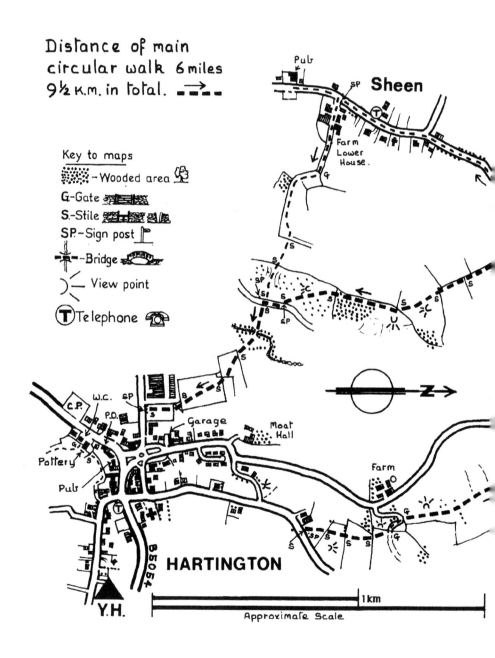

Distance of main circular walk 6 miles 9½ k.m. in total.

Key to maps
- Wooded area
- G-Gate
- S.-Stile
- SP.-Sign post
- -Bridge
- View point
- T Telephone

1 km
Approximate Scale

116

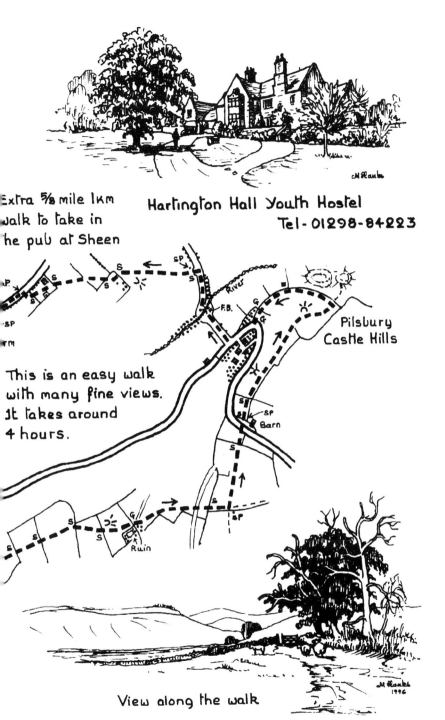

Extra ⅝ mile 1km walk to take in the pub at Sheen

Hartington Hall Youth Hostel
Tel - 01298-84223

River

F.B.

Pilsbury Castle Hills

This is an easy walk with many fine views. It takes around 4 hours.

Barn

SP

Ruin

View along the walk

Map 47
Hartington, Biggin Dale and Wolfscote Dale
see page 103

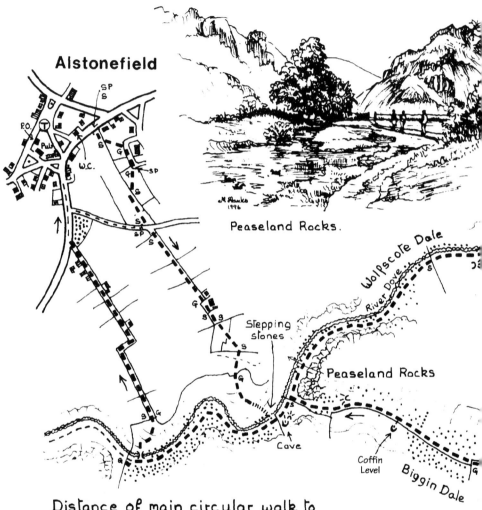

Peaseland Rocks.

Distance of main circular walk to
Peaseland Rocks 6 miles 9½ km in total
and takes around 4 hours.
For the section on to Alstonefield add an
extra 3 miles 4¾ km in total.

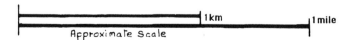

Approximate Scale

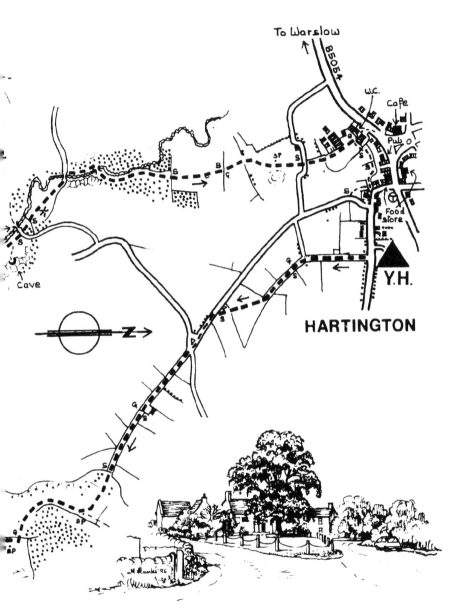

To Warslow

B5054

W.C.

Cafe

Pub

Food store

Y.H.

HARTINGTON

Cave

Z →

Part of the attractive village of Alstonefield

Map 48
Hartington YH to Youlgreave YH: 1
see page 103

Hartington Hall Youth Hostel
Tel - 01298 - 84223

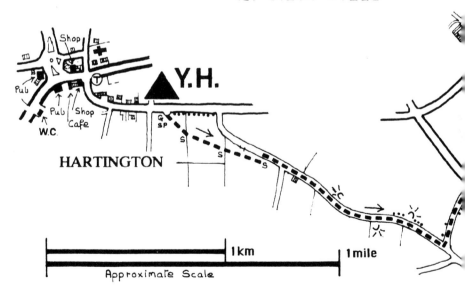

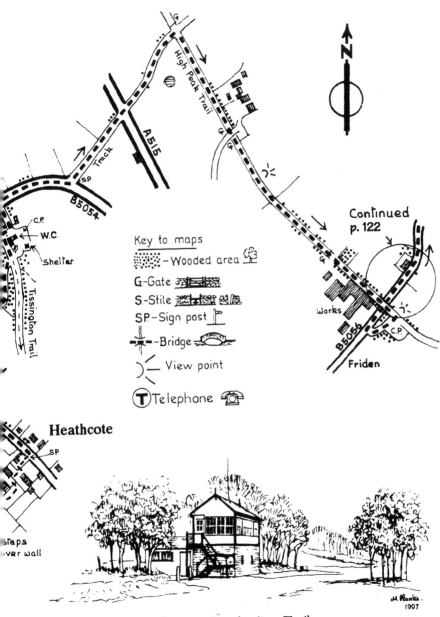

High Peak Trail

A515

SP Track

B5054

C.P.
W.C.
Shelter

Tissington Trail

G

G

Key to maps

░ —Wooded area 🌳
G–Gate
S.–Stile
S.P.–Sign post
✛ –Bridge
)(– View point
Ⓣ Telephone ☎

Continued
p. 122

G

Works

B5058

C.P.

Friden

Heathcote

SP

Steps
over wall

M. Planks.
1907

Information centre on Tissington Trail

121

Map 49
Hartington YH to Youlgreave YH: 2
see page 103

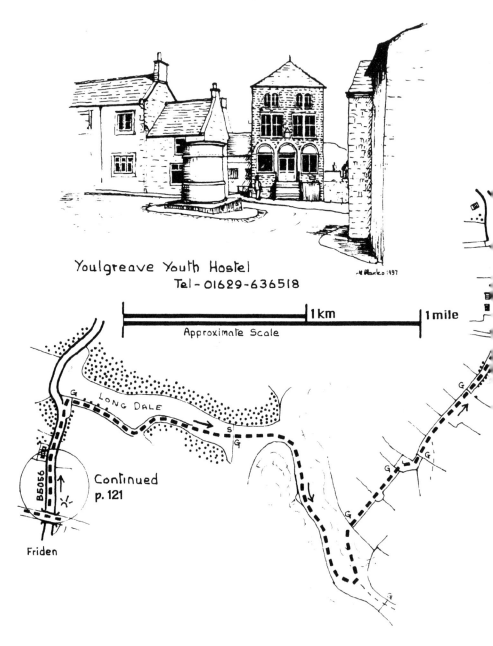

Youlgreave Youth Hostel
Tel - 01629 - 636518

1 km   1 mile
Approximate Scale

LONG DALE

B5056

Continued
p. 121

Friden

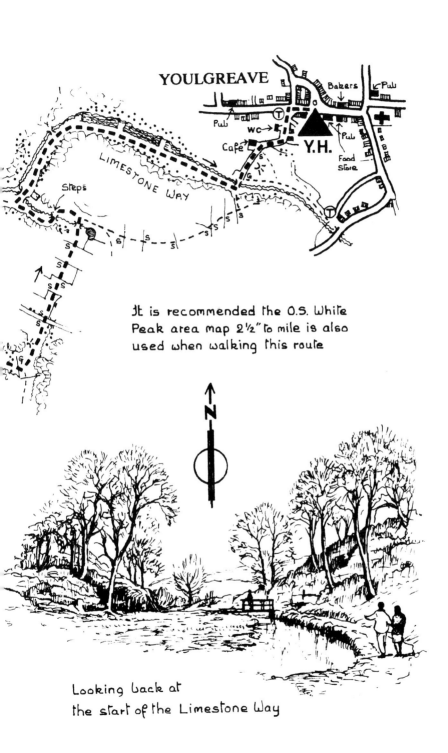

YOULGREAVE

Bakers

Pub

Pub

wc

Cafe

Y.H.

Food Store

Pub

LIMESTONE WAY

Steps

It is recommended the O.S. White Peak area map 2½" to mile is also used when walking this route

N

Looking back at
the start of the Limestone Way

Walks around Bakewell (OS Outdoor Leisure Map 24)

Bakewell to Chatsworth 8.5 miles (13.5km)
Map 50 (see pages 128 / 129)

Walk out of town, over the river and onto the old railway station, now the start of the Monsal Trail. Walk up the path close to the golf course. It enters a wood, emerging by Ballcross Farm. Turn right on the road and then right down the old Bakewell-Edensor road to Edensor village. All the houses here were built in different styles, yet they remain surprisingly harmonious. A notice in the church explains how the village came to be removed to its current site. Sir Joseph Paxton and Kathleen Kennedy (the sister of President J F Kennedy) are buried here.

Continue on to Chatsworth. Allow a couple of hours at least to see the house and perhaps as long again for the garden. Return down the west bank of the River Derwent through the park to Calton Lees before heading back via Calton Pastures and Manners Wood to Bakewell. Look out for the Russian Cottage — a log cabin given by Tsar Nicholas I to the Duke of Devonshire in 1844. Although visible from the path, unfortunately it is on private land.

Bakewell to Lathkill Dale & Haddon Hall
Map 51 (see pages 130 / 131) 7.5 miles (12km)

This route takes you down part of Lathkill Dale, one of the prettiest of the Derbyshire dales, before returning via medieval Haddon Hall.

Climb out of the town up past Lady Manners School before reaching the quiet village of Over Haddon with its Craft Centre (worth a visit). From the pub (The Lathkill Hotel) take the path which drops down the fields to Conksbury Bridge. Cross the latter and turn left to follow the River Lathkill downstream. At Coalpit Bridge turn left and go directly to Haddon Hall if you wish to spend time there. Otherwise continue down the dale to Alport and then take the path across the fields to Haddon Hall. Alternatively use the bus if the timing is right — there's a bus stop in Alport — alighting at Haddon Hall.

Visit the hall as required and then return to Bakewell through the river meadows. Alternatively, check the bus times and return to Bakewell on the bus.

Bakewell YH to Buxton YH (OS Outdoor Leisure Map 24)
Maps 52 / 53 (see pages 132 / 135) 13 miles (21km)

A long but rewarding walk along one of the finest Derbyshire Dales to Monyash. Thereafter the walk continues across the plateau to reach Buxton.

Leave Fly Hill, pass the church and over the B5055, proceeding out of town and through the school grounds before turning left onto the Portway, one of the oldest tracks which crossed the Peak. After a short distance, the Portway continues to Alport, but our path turns right and uphill, heading for Over Haddon. It has a good pub but you should be too early for that!

Descend into Lathkill Dale, now a National Nature Reserve. The southern bank is in shade and has a different habitat to the north side of the river. Look out for the remains of Mandale Lead Mine which closed in 1852, together with the aquaduct piers which supported a water trough bringing water to a mine waterwheel. The River Lathkill is crystal clear with trout readily visible.

At Cales Dale the route turns left to leave the dale, but you can continue directly up Lathkill

Dale to Monyash if you prefer a slight short-cut. Our route goes via One Ash Grange and then along the Oldway between Youlgreave and Monyash. In the latter, there is a cafe and pub (The Bulls Head) side by side facing the village green. Sir Maurice Oldfield is buried at the church — he was the basis for 'M' in the James Bond movies. Look out for the village pond or mere. There used to be four here in times gone by.

Leaving the village, the path cuts across the little fields on the plateau to reach Flagg and then Chelmorton. From here the path is the same one as in the Ravenstor-Buxton walk and heads directly across the fields to Buxton.

Walks around Youlgreave (OS Outdoor Leisure Map 24)

Youlgreave to Haddon Hall 5.5 miles (8.75km)
Map 54 (see pages 136 / 137)

This path takes you to a short stretch of Lathkill Dale. It goes on to Haddon Hall before returning via Bradford Dale to Youlgreave.

Walk to the church and bear right, turning left at the signpost and heading for Alport. Turn up Lathkill Dale and follow the river meadows. It is a pleasant stroll on a popular path. Soon Raper Lodge is passed (to your left). This lovely house — plus Youlgreave and the old Co-Op, now the youth hostel — featured in the film 'The Virgin and the Gypsy' written by D H Lawrence. Lawrence lived at nearby Middleton-by-Wirksworth during the Great War with his German wife, Frieda.

Cross the old bridge below Raper Lodge called Coalpit Bridge. Climb out of the valley and go along the track. Soon a lovely view of sixteenth-century Haddon Hall is directly in front of you.

Return across the fields to Bradford Dale which is followed back to Youlgreave. The circular stone tank opposite the youth hostel dates from 1829 and was part of the village's water supply, although it is now no longer used. The new supply in 1829 was marked by a celebration dressing of the wells with flower petals pressed into clay. This still happens in June (ask the warden for details); Youlgreave is regarded as one of the better examples of this well-dressing custom.

Youlgreave to Robin Hood's Stride

Youlgreave to Gratton Dale
Map 55 (see page 138 / 139)
These two circular walks are described under **Walks around Elton**. Note also the short evening walk shown on the map which goes down the River Bradford on the far side of the river. It may be extended as part of a figure of eight, going up Bradford Dale, then left up the steps and back across the fields as shown on the map.

Walks around Elton

Elton to Youlgreave and Robin Hood's Stride

Map 56 (see pages 140 / 141)   7 miles (11km)

This route also serves as the **inter-hostel route to Youlgreave YH**. It crosses rolling countryside to reach lovely Bradford Dale and its clear trout stream. From Youlgreave, the return path leaves the limestone and climbs up onto Harthill Moor past a stone circle and Iron Age fort to return to Elton.

From the hostel, head towards the church and take the path to Dale Head, a small hamlet on the Elton to Middleton-by-Youlgreave road. From here the path cuts through the fields towards Bradford Dale. It has several clear pools before Youlgreave is reached. Turn left up into the village if required.

The path leaves the dale here and climbs gradually up onto Harthill Moor, now pastureland. As you cross the lane having reached Harthill Moor Farm, look for the remaining standing stones of Nine Stones Stone Circle (some of the original stones are now missing). By the rock formation known as Robin Hood's Stride, a short path crosses on your left to the Hermit's Cave which makes a quick but interesting detour. The path to the cave passes the edge of an Iron Age encampment.

From here its a short walk back to Elton, reaching the village by the church.

Elton to Gratton Dale

Map 56 (see pages 140 / 141)   6.75 miles (10.75km)

A short circular route taking in the little-known Gratton Dale and returning on two paths which formed part of former important routeways, now almost forgotten.

Go past the church to where the road bears off to the right. Continue on a path past Oddo House Farm to reach Gratton Dale. Proceed up the dale, bearing right after about a mile. The dale (or valley) shallows considerably; where it swings around to the north it joins the Peakway, a medieval road which ran up through the Peak District and now is virtually unknown.

Our path leaves this by turning right into a shallow valley, the headwaters of the streams which flow to Bradford Dale. The path turns upstream back towards Elton on the old Manchester to Derby main road. You have to stretch your imagination a bit now to appreciate its former importance — the route was overtaken by the turnpike system when the line of the road was re-routed to an easier gradient on what is now the Ashbourne-Buxton road.

The path proceeds across the fields along the line of the old road to Dale End where it is tarred and still in use. Either follow the road to Elton or take the preferred route, a path which cuts up the fields to the left of the road to Elton church.

Elton to Winster & Birchover

Map 57 (see pages 142 / 143)

5.5 miles (8.75km)

This route heads eastwards to the old mining village of Winster, then north to Birchover and back to Elton. It is a varied route with some good scenery.

Leave Elton, heading east from the village along the road to the B5056 (ie turn right on leaving the youth hostel). Turn right after half a mile on a farm track and then turn left heading directly to Winster. Look out for the hall and the market hall in the main street. The latter was the first building to be purchased in Derbyshire by the National Trust. It is now a shop and information centre.

Turn left just before the market hall on a path heading for Birchover. It cuts through a small wood and gains ground on the way. The Druid Inn in the village keeps good food and beer. The path takes the lane in front of the pub skirting Rowter Rocks before crossing the B5056 to Robin Hood's Stride. It returns to Elton on the **path to Youlgreave** mentioned above.

Notice that the map shows other alternative paths you can use.

Three Shires Head.

Map 50
Bakewell to Chatsworth
see page 124

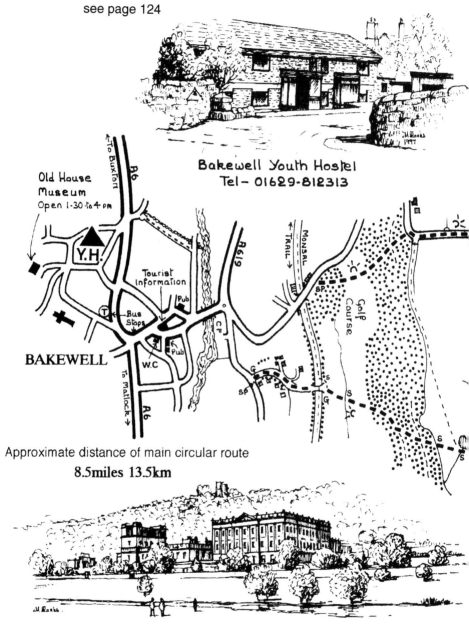

Bakewell Youth Hostel
Tel- 01629-812313

Old House Museum
Open 1·30 to 4 pm

Y.H.

Tourist Information

Pub

Bus Stops

Pub

BAKEWELL

W.C

Golf Course

Approximate distance of main circular route

8.5miles 13.5km

Chatsworth House.

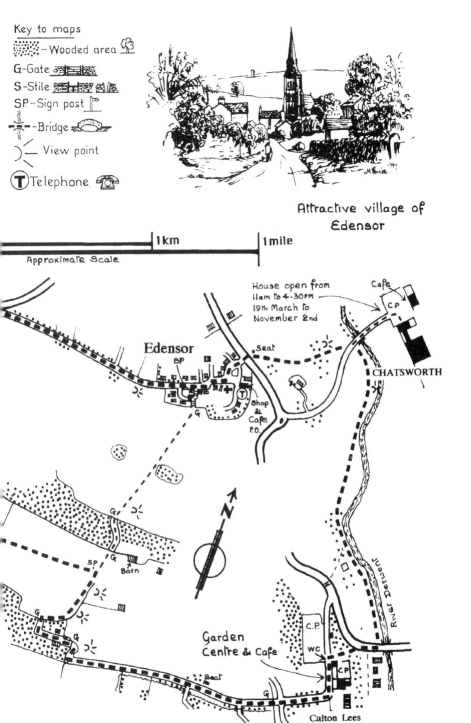

Key to maps

- :::::: –Wooded area
- G–Gate
- S–Stile
- S.P.–Sign post
- –Bridge
- View point
- T Telephone

Attractive village of
Edensor

1km   1mile

Approximate Scale

House open from
11am to 4·30pm
19th March to
November 2nd

Cafe
CP

Edensor
SP

Seat

CHATSWORTH

T

Shop
&
Cafe
P.O.

G

N

Gr

SP
Barn

G

River Derwent

C.P.

WC

G

Garden
Centre & Cafe

C.P

Seat

G

Calton Lees

129

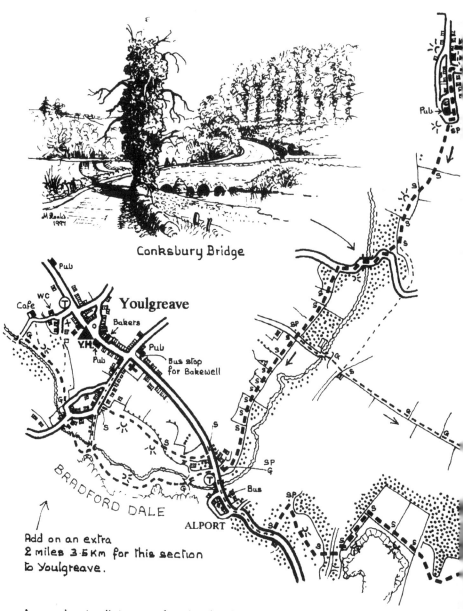

Conksbury Bridge

Pub

Cafe WC Youlgreave

Bakers

YH Pub

Pub Bus stop for Bakewell

BRADFORD DALE

Add on an extra
2 miles 3.5 Km for this section
to Youlgreave.

SP

Bus

ALPORT

Approximate distance of main circular route

7.5 miles, 12 Km ▪ ▪ ▪ ▪

|———————————————|1km |1 mile

Map 51
Bakewell to Lathkill Dale and Haddon Hall
see page 124

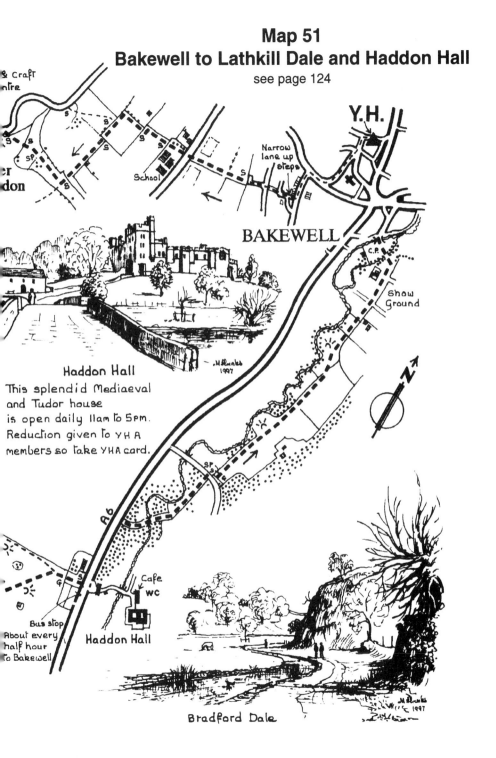

& Craft
ntre

Y.H.

Narrow
lane up
steps

School

er
don

BAKEWELL

C.P.

Snow
Ground

Haddon Hall

This splendid Mediaeval
and Tudor house
is open daily 11am to 5pm.
Reduction given to Y H A
members so take YHA card.

A6

Cafe
WC

Bus stop
About every
half hour
to Bakewell

Haddon Hall

Bradford Dale

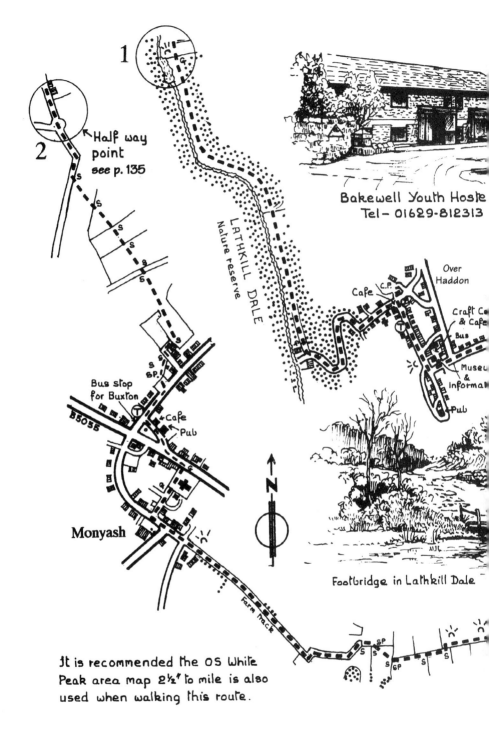

1

2

Half way point
see p. 135

LATHKILL DALE
Nature reserve

Bakewell Youth Hostel
Tel - 01629-812313

Over Haddon

Cafe C.P.

Craft Ce & Cafe

Bus

Museu & Informa

Pub

Cafe

Bus stop for Buxton

B5055

Cafe

Pub

Monyash

N

Farm Track

Footbridge in Lathkill Dale

It is recommended the OS White Peak area map 2½" to mile is also used when walking this route.

132

Map 52
Bakewell YH to Buxton YH: 1
see page 124

Approximate distance 13 miles 21 km

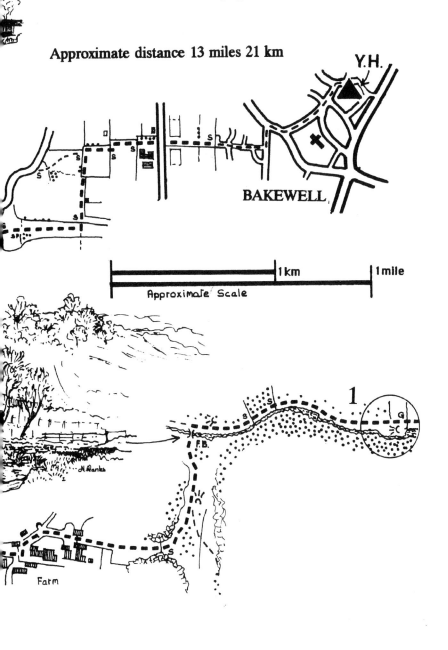

Y.H.

BAKEWELL

1km 1mile

Approximate Scale

N Planks

1

Farm

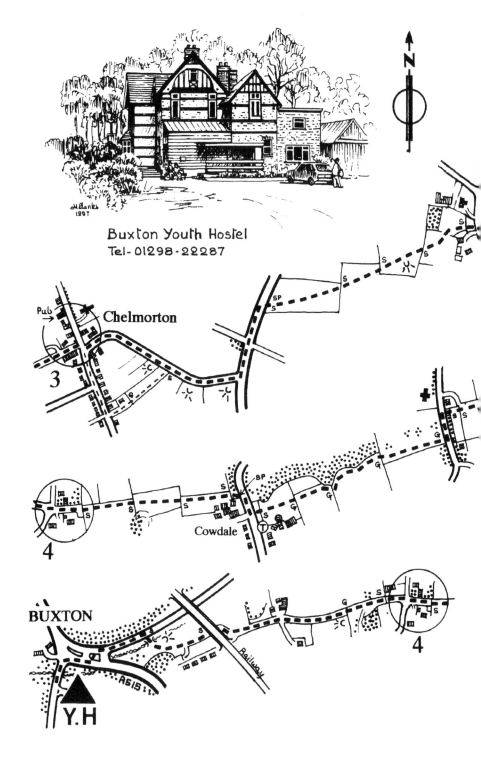

Buxton Youth Hostel
Tel- 01298·22287

Chelmorton

Pub

3

4

Cowdale

BUXTON

Railway

A515

Y.H

4

Map 53
Bakewell YH to Buxton YH: 2
see page 124

Half way point
see p. 132

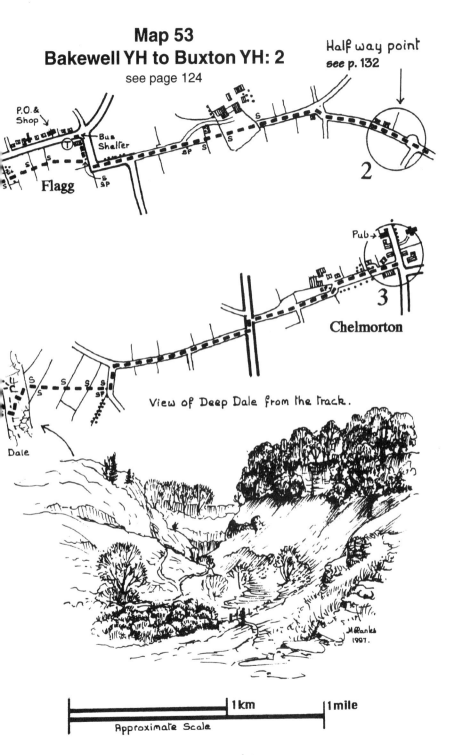

P.O. & Shop

Bus Shelter

Flagg

2

Pub→

3

Chelmorton

Dale

View of Deep Dale from the track.

M.Ranks
1997.

1km   1mile

Approximate Scale

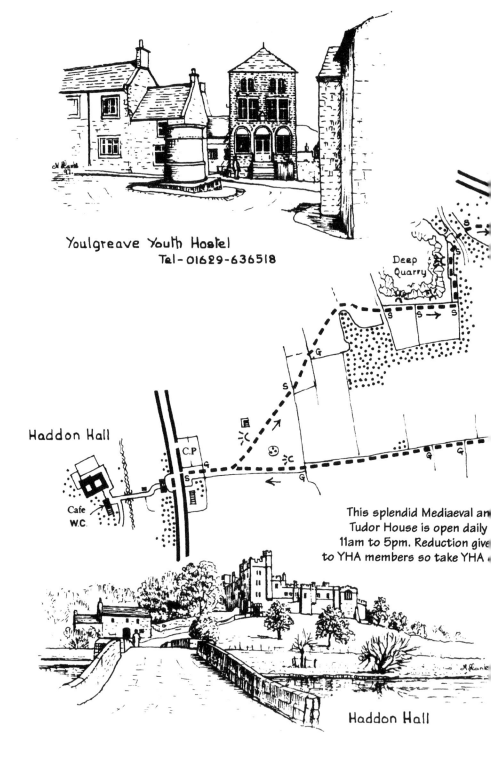

Youlgreave Youth Hostel
Tel- 01629-636518

Deep Quarry

Haddon Hall

C.P

Cafe
W.C.

This splendid Mediaeval an
Tudor House is open daily
11am to 5pm. Reduction give
to YHA members so take YHA

Haddon Hall

Map 54
Youlgreave to Haddon Hall
see page 125

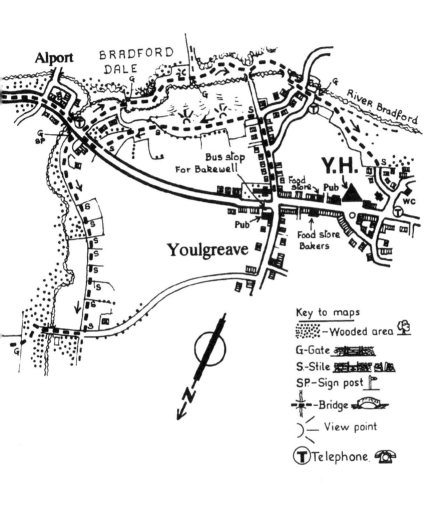

Alport

BRADFORD DALE

River Bradford

Bus stop For Bakewell

Y.H.

Food Store

Pub

WC

Pub

Food store Bakers

Youlgreave

Key to maps

⠿ — Wooded area 🌳

G-Gate

S.-Stile

SP-Sign post

▬ — Bridge

View point

Ⓣ Telephone ☎

Approximate distance of main circular
route 5.5 miles 8.75 km in total

| | 1 km | 1 mile |

Approximate Scale

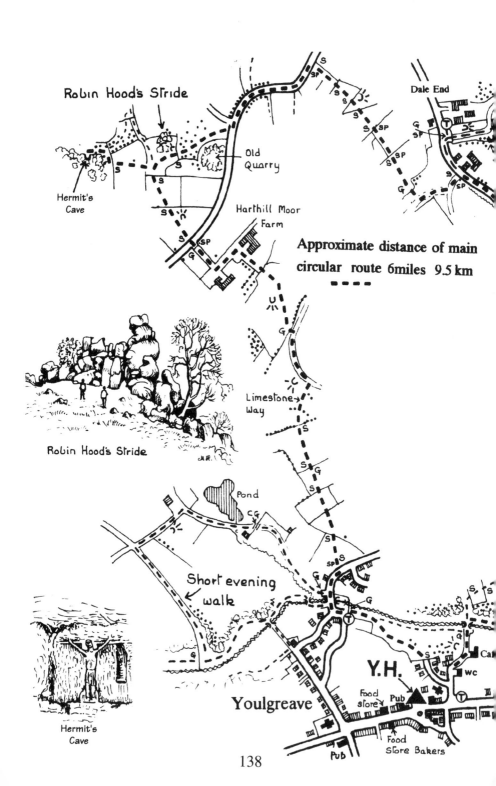

Robin Hood's Stride

Hermit's Cave

Old Quarry

Dale End

Harthill Moor Farm

Approximate distance of main circular route 6miles 9.5 km

- - - -

Robin Hood's Stride

Limestone Way

Pond

Short evening walk

Hermit's Cave

Youlgreave

Y.H.

Food store

Pub

Food Store Bakers

Pub

138

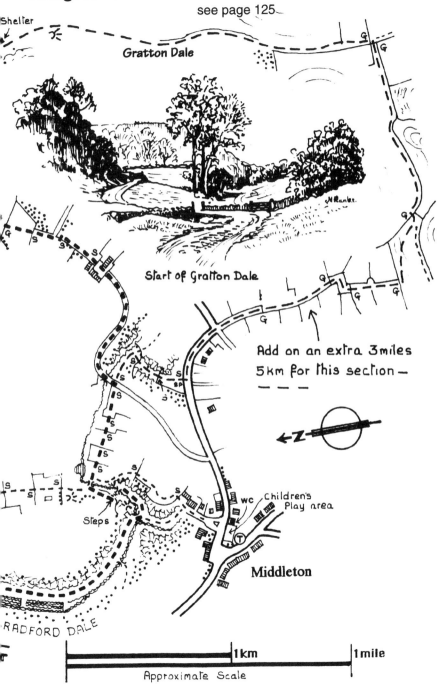

Shelter

Gratton Dale

Start of Gratton Dale

Add on an extra 3 miles
5 km for this section —

wc Children's
Play area

Steps

Middleton

RADFORD DALE

1 km   1 mile

Approximate Scale

Map 56
Elton to Youlgreave and Robin Hood's Stride
see page 126

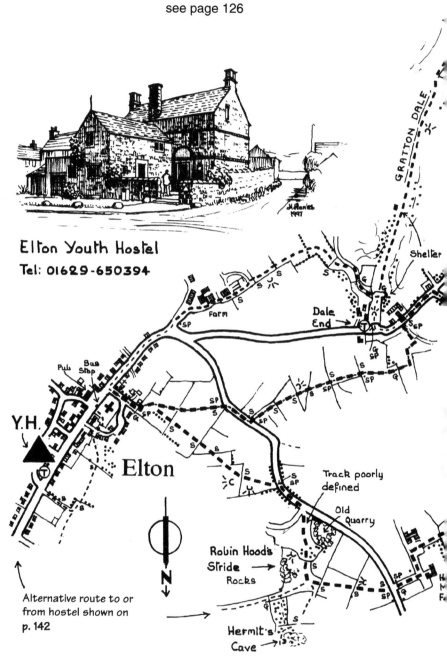

Elton Youth Hostel
Tel: 01629-650394

GRATTON DALE

Shelter

Farm

Dale End →

Pub

Bus Stop

Y.H.

Elton

N

Track poorly defined

Old Quarry

Robin Hood's Stride →
Rocks

Alternative route to or from hostel shown on p. 142

Hermit's Cave

140

Approximate distance of main
circular route to Youlgreave
7miles 11km in total - - - -

Gratton Dale route
6.75miles 10.75km in total

- - - - - -■■-

to map

- Wooded area
Gate
Stile
- Sign post
- Bridge
- View point

Telephone

Middleton

River
Bradford

Steps

Weir

Youlgreave

Cafe
W.C.
Pub

YH
Pub
Food
Store
Food
Store
Pub

Youlgreave Church

1km   1mile

Approximate Scale

141

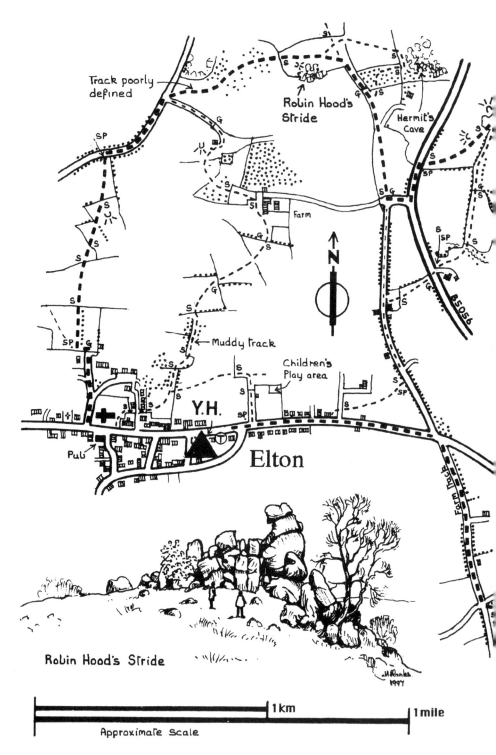

Track poorly
defined

Robin Hood's
Stride

Hermit's
Cave

Farm

N

Muddy track

Children's
Play area

Y.H.

Pub

Elton

Farm Track

Robin Hood's Stride

1km

1mile

Approximate Scale

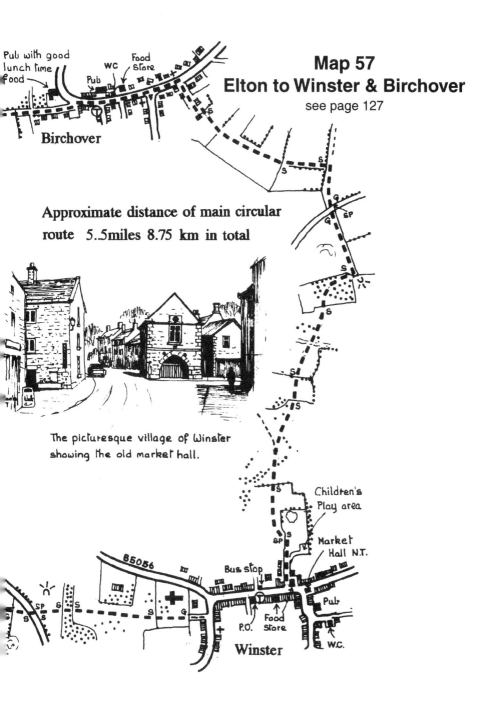

Map 57
Elton to Winster & Birchover
see page 127

Pub with good lunch time food

WC Food Store

Pub

Birchover

Approximate distance of main circular route 5..5miles 8.75 km in total

The picturesque village of Winster showing the old market hall.

Children's Play area

Market Hall N.T.

B5056

Bus stop

SP

Pub

P.O.   Food Store

Winster

W.C.

143

Walks around Matlock

Matlock YH to Elton YH & Youlgreave YH   (OS Outdoor Leisure Map 24)

Matlock YH to Elton YH 6.5 miles (10.5km) / Matlock YH to Youlgreave YH 8miles-
(12.5km)

Maps 58 / 59 (see pages 148 / 151)

This route follows the River Derwent before climbing out of the valley to head for Birchover. From here, the route splits to go north-west or south-west, depending on your destination.

Descend the street Bank Road, cross the bridge and turn right. The route follows the river past the railway station and the Peak Rail preserved railway terminus. It heads for (but skirts around the east side of) Oaker Hill, a small rounded hill with a single tree on the top. There were once two trees planted here by two brothers who then parted, never to see each other again.

Once past the hill, at the church the path reaches Darley Bridge village. Turn left up the road for a short distance and then turn right to head for a lead smelting works. This is situated next to the site of Millclose Mine, abandoned in 1938 but once the most important lead mine in England.

The path now turns west along an old lane which runs to the south of Birchover. Look out for the restored stocks, and divert into the village if you require lunch. It is only about a mile from here to Elton across the fields, although you could take the Youlgreave track to Robin Hood's Stride and then go southwards to Elton as shown on the map.

If you are heading for Youlgreave, cross the B5056 and take the track which goes between Robin Hood's Stride and the Hermit's Cave. The path heads for Harthill Moor Farm. Look at the standing stones to your right. They are the remains of a former stone circle known as Nine Stones Circle. From the farm, the path heads downhill towards the lovely Bradford Dale and the village of Youlgreave.

Matlock YH to Shining Cliff YH   (OS Outdoor Leisure Map 24)
Maps 60 / 61 (see pages 152 / 155)   8.5 miles (13km)

The route climbs out of Matlock to Riber Castle (where there are marvellous views) before descending to High Peak Junction and a walk along a disused canal — now a nature reserve. This route includes some important centres of industrial history. Alternatively, garden lovers may prefer a detour to Lea Gardens.

Descend to the bottom of Bank Road and walk through the park on your left. The shelter is the old Crown Square tram shelter. Bank Road had a street tram operating on a similar principle to that of the San Francisco trams. Leave the park and head uphill past the church (usually locked) to reach the school. Turn left and climb uphill to Riber Castle, now a reserve for rare British breeds. The path then heads through fields and woodland to reach Lea Bridge.

The textile mill here (mill shop available) is Smedleys, but was once owned by Florence Nightingale's father. She lived nearby. If you wish to divert to Lea Garden, take the road which runs through the factory and climb up for about a mile. Lea Garden on the right has a collection of some 500 different rhododendron species. There is a tearoom there too.

From Lea Bridge, the path heads down to the Cromford Canal and High Peak Junction. The building with a tall chimney contains the largest surviving steam-operated plunger pump in the country. It is worked by a beam engine with a 30 ft long beam. The 60-inch steam cylinder dates from 1849. At High Peak Junction is the incline where wagons were hauled by steam up the Cromford and High Peak Railway. A steam-operated winder is preserved at Middleton-by-

Wirksworth and is open to the public, as is the Lea Wood pumping engine (check the Tourist Information Centre at Matlock Bath for opening/steaming arrangements).

High Peak Junction railway workshop buildings include the oldest in-situ railway line in the world — dating from 1825; old wagons; the incline catchpit and a small book shop of railway-related titles.

If you are interested in industrial history, there is much to see in Cromford village where the Arkwright Mill is being restored. The village has lots of surviving links with Sir Richard Arkwright.

From High Peak Junction, follow the canal tow-path to Whatstandwell, before climbing out of the valley through Alderwasley Park to reach Shining Cliff Y H.

Matlock to Bonsall & Matlock Bath

(OS Outdoor Leisure Map)

Map 62 (see pages 156 / 157)   5.5 miles (8.75km)

From the bottom of Bank Road, climb up the fields out of the Derwent valley to reach the small village of Bonsall and its distinctive cross. From here it is a short walk across the fields before dropping down into Matlock Bath, emerging on the A6 by Gulliver's Kingdom (for small children); the Peak District Mining Museum; the Matlock Bath Tourist Information Centre; and Temple Mine, an old lead mine open to visitors.

Walk to where the cable car starts (near the railway station). You can take the cable car to the Heights of Abraham from here if you wish. Otherwise, climb out of the valley to High Tor before descending back into Matlock by the church. There is a very good view of Matlock from the war memorial in the churchyard.

Matlock to Lea Bridge, Cromford & Matlock Bath

Map 63 (see pages 158 / 159)   8 miles (12.5km)

This route follows the **inter hostel route to Shining Cliff YH** as far as High Peak Wharf. From here, walk along the canal to Cromford Wharf & Arkwright's Mill. Explore Cromford before walking alongside the A6 to Matlock Bath. It passes another of Arkwright's mills en-route.

From Matlock Bath, return on the route via High Tor mentioned above.

Walks around Shining Cliff

(OS Outdoor Leisure Map 24)

Map 64 (see pages 160 / 161)   7.75 miles (12.5km)

A walk to Crich village to the National Tramway Museum. Although the recommended return route is via Alderwasley Park, an easy route incorporating a disused canal (now a nature reserve) is an alternative option.

Descend through the wood to Ambergate and turn left on the A6, following the road past the Little Chef before turning right. Cross the railway and canal bridges and then climb up the wooded valleyside. It is just over 1 mile to reach the edge of Crich village. Proceed to the National Tramway Museum which has over 50 trams, lovingly restored. Several operate, so you can enjoy the experience of a tramride. There is a museum, cafe and a re-created street scene here to provide the necessary setting for the trams. You can also explore the garages where the trams are stored.

From here, descend back into the Derwent Valley at Whatstandwell. If you wish to take the alternative route, turn left along the canal towpath. Otherwise, cross the valley by following the A6 across the old stonebuilt bridge. Climb out of the valley, turning left to reach Alderwasley Park and the top of Shining Cliff Wood. North of the youth hostel, but currently off a public right of way, the wood includes an old yew tree. A family used to live in it — and it is the origin of the nursery rhyme *Rock a bye baby in the tree top*.

Camping Barns

The majority of the networks of Camping Barns in England incorporate a YHA Booking Bureau. This operates in the Peak District in respect of twelve camping barns. These are watertight barns offering simple accommodation only.

They are situated at: Abney, near Eyam; Birchover; Butterton (two barns); Edale; Losehill near Castleton; Middleton-by-Youlgreave; Nab End near Longnor; Ash Grange near Youlgreave; Taddington; Wildboarclough; and Upper Booth, Edale.

The booking office is:

Camping Barns Reservations Office,
16 Shawbridge St, Clitheroe, Lancs BB7 1LY
☎ 01200 428366

A leaflet *Camping Barns in England* is also available from YHA, 8 St Stephens Hill, St Albans, Herts AL1 2DY
☎ 01727 845047

E-mail:

yhacustomerservices@compuserve.com
http://www.yha-england-wales.org.uk

Rent a Hostel

Out of season, many Youth Hostels are available for rent in their entirety. Rent a Hostel is popular, so book in plenty of time. You get exclusive use of the building. All bed linen, kitchen equipment, lighting and heating is provided. In some hostels, but not in the Peak District, even the catering can be taken care of.

Call YHA for a brochure on 01727 845047 or, to make a booking, ☎ 01722 337494.

Castleton:

The Old Vicarage, adjacent to Castleton Hall YH.
Eight bedrooms with 28 bunk beds (1x1, 1x2, 5x4, 1x5). All rooms have ensuite shower and toilet. Building decorated to a very high standard.

The Castleton Hall Barn:

Behind the Old Hall. Eight bedrooms with 40 bunk beds (2x2, 5x4, 1x16). All rooms have wash handbasins. Only suitable for maximum 36, due to size of dining room.

Bretton:

* 3 bedrooms with 18 bunk beds (1x4, 1x6, 1x8).

Crowden:

8 bedrooms with 50 beds but only suitable for 40 owing to capacity of kitchen.

Meerbrook:

* 5 bedrooms with 22 bunk beds (2x2, 1x4 with adjoining 1x6, 1x8).

Dimmingsdale:

* 3 bedrooms with 20 bunk beds (2x6, 1x8).

Shining Cliff:

5 bedrooms with 26 bunk beds (2x4, 3x6). This youth hostel has no showers and only simple accommodation.

* **Non smoking youth hostel.**

Approximate distance of main routes
Matlock - Elton 6.5miles 10.5 km
Matlock - Youlgreave 8miles 12.5 km

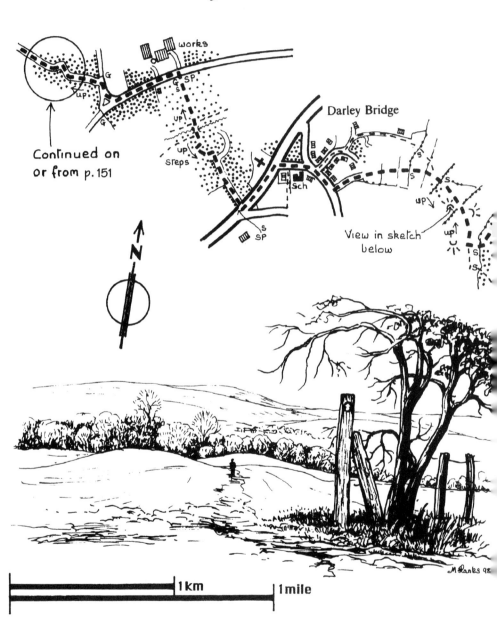

works

G

SP

up

Continued on
or from p. 151

Darley Bridge

up

up

steps

Sch

S
SP

up

View in sketch
below

up

N

1 km   1 mile

M Planks 95

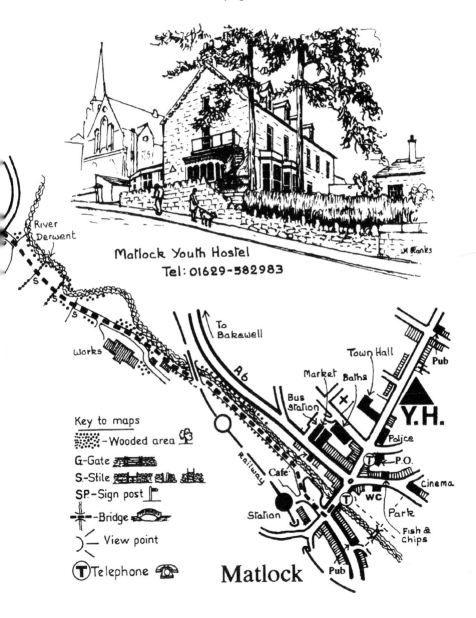

Matlock Youth Hostel
Tel: 01629-582983

River Derwent

Works

To Bakewell

A6

Town Hall

Market   Baths

Pub

Bus Station

Y.H.

Police

T — P.O.

Cinema

T   WC

Park

Fish & Chips

Railway

Cafe

Station

Matlock

Pub

Key to maps

- Wooded area
- G-Gate
- S-Stile
- SP.-Sign post
- Bridge
- View point
- (T) Telephone

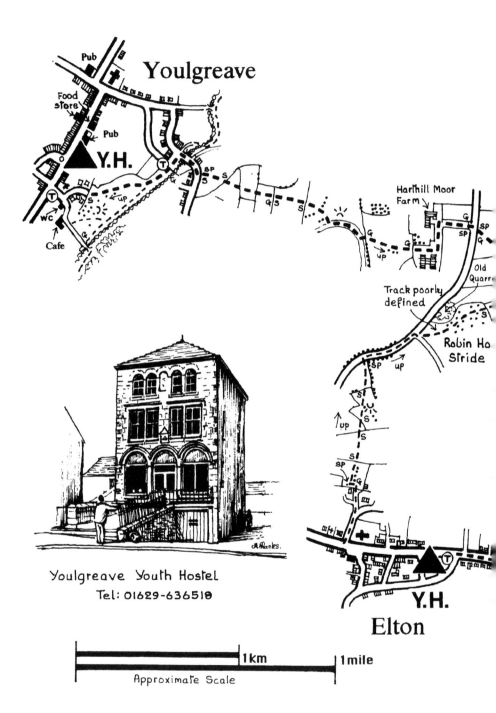

Youlgreave

Harthill Moor Farm

Old Quarry

Track poorly defined

Robin Ho Stride

Youlgreave Youth Hostel
Tel: 01629-636518

Elton

Y.H.

1km   1mile

Approximate Scale

Map 59
Matlock YH to Elton YH and Youlgreave YH: 2
see page 144

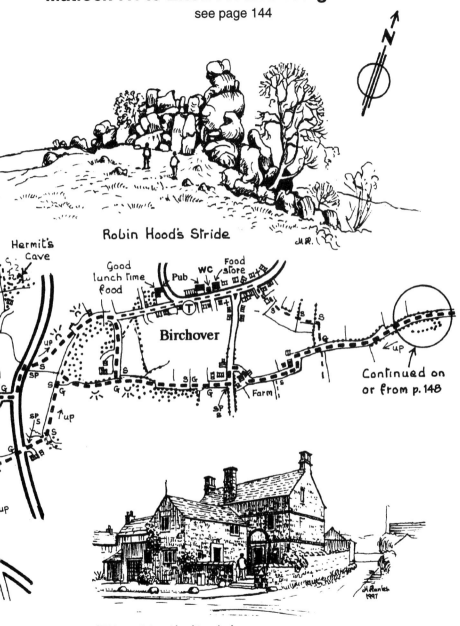

Robin Hood's Stride

Hermit's Cave

Good lunch time food

Pub WC Food store

Birchover

Farm

Continued on
or from p. 148

Elton Youth Hostel
Tel: 01629-650394

Map 60
Matlock YH to Shining Cliff YH: 1
see page 144

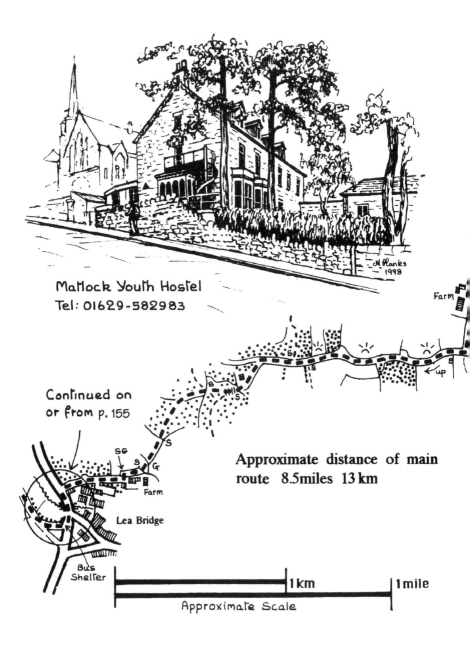

Matlock Youth Hostel
Tel: 01629-582983

M Planks
1998

Farm

Continued on
or from p. 155

up

SG

G

Farm

Lea Bridge

Approximate distance of main route 8.5miles 13 km

Bus
Shelter

1km   1mile

Approximate Scale

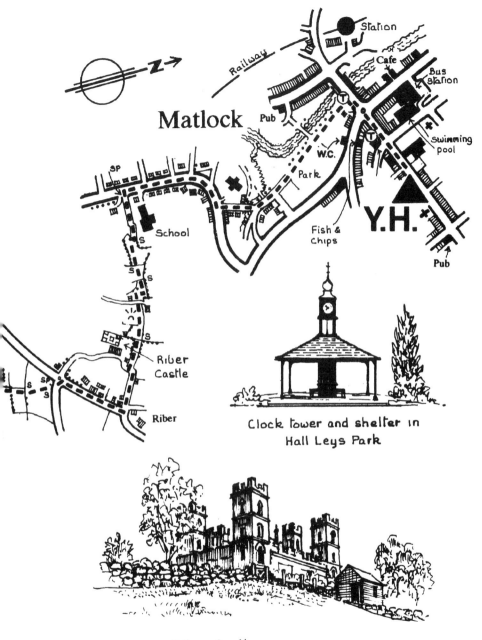

Matlock

Clock tower and shelter in
Hall Leys Park

Riber Castle
19th century folly now a fauna reserve & wildlife
Park for rare breeds

Map 61
Matlock YH to Shining Cliff YH: 2
see page 144

Alderwasley Park

Shining Cliff

Y.H

Farm

Farm

Cross in Alderwasley Park

Station

Pub

Whatstandwell

Shining Cliff Youth Hostel

N.Banks
1998.

1km

1mile

Approximate Scale

154

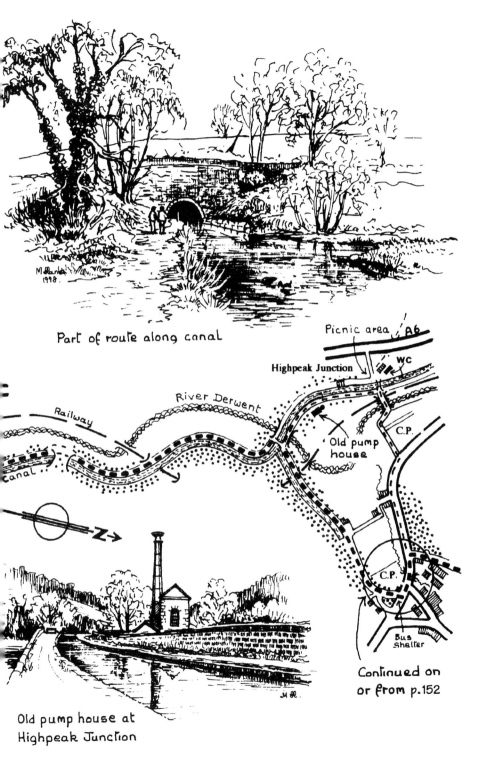

Part of route along canal

Picnic area / A6

Highpeak Junction

WC

River Derwent

Railway

Old pump house

C.P.

canal

Z→

C.P.

Bus Shelter

Continued on or from p.152

Old pump house at Highpeak Junction

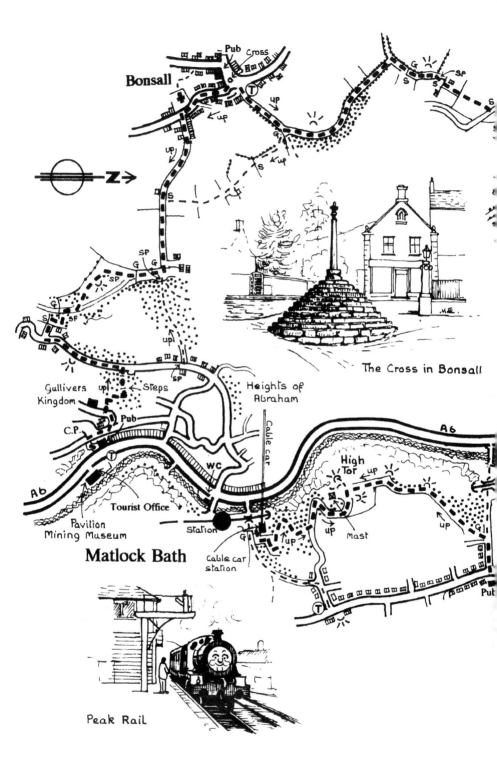

Bonsall

The Cross in Bonsall

Gullivers Kingdom

Heights of Abraham

Cable car

High Tor

Mast

Steps

Pub

C.P.

Tourist Office

Pavilion Mining Museum

WC

Station

Cable car station

Matlock Bath

Peak Rail

Map 62
Matlock to Bonsall and Matlock Bath
see page 145

Matlock Youth Hostel
Tel: 01629-582983

Approximate distance of main circular route 5.5 miles 8.75 km

1 km   1 mile

Approximate Scale

157

Map 63
Matlock to Lea Bridge, Cromford and Matlock Bath
see page 145

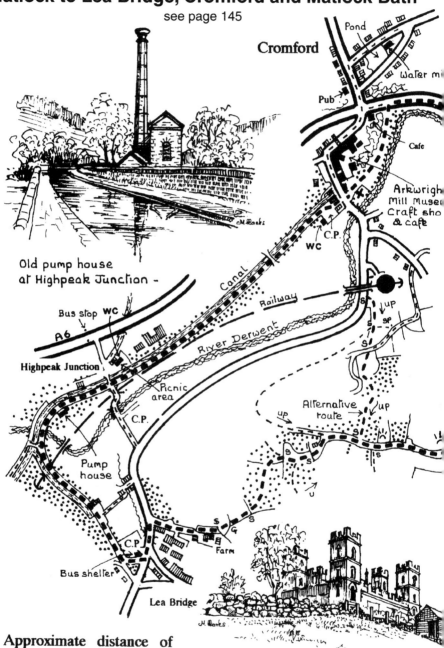

Cromford

Pond

Water m

Pub

Cafe

Arkwrigh
Mill Muse
Craft sho
& cafe

C.P.
WC

Old pump house
at Highpeak Junction -

Canal

Railway

Bus stop WC

A6

River Derwent

Highpeak Junction

Picnic
area

up
Alternative
route
up

up

C.P.

Pump
house

S
G
S

C.P.

Farm

Bus shelter

Lea Bridge

River Castle
19th century folly now a fauna

Approximate distance of
main circular route
8 miles   12.5 km

158

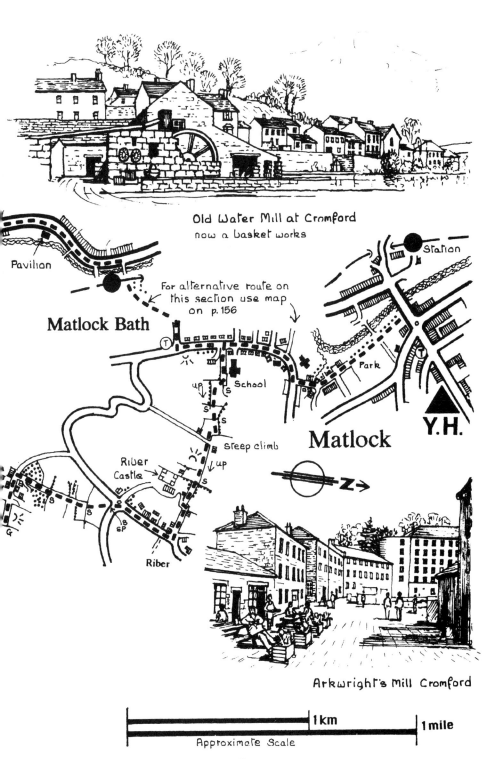

Old Water Mill at Cromford
now a basket works

Pavilion

Station

For alternative route on
this section use map
on p. 156

Matlock Bath

School

Park

up
S
S
S

Steep climb

Matlock

Y.H.

Riber
Castle

up
S

G

SP

Riber

→Z→

Arkwright's Mill Cromford

1km | 1mile

Approximate Scale

Map 64
Shining Cliff to the National Tramway Museum, Crich

see page 145

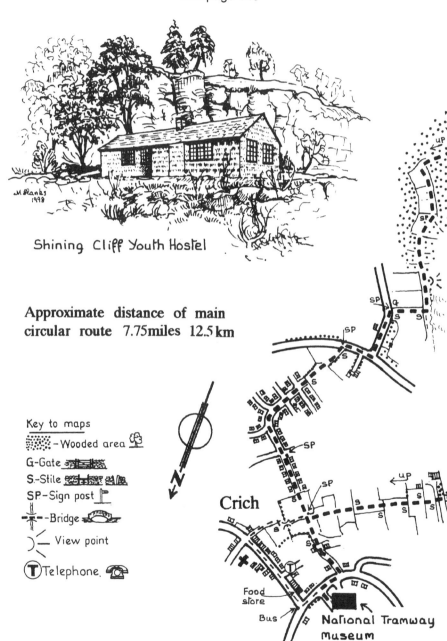

Shining Cliff Youth Hostel

Approximate distance of main
circular route 7.75 miles 12.5 km

Key to maps
:::::: – Wooded area
G–Gate
S.–Stile
SP–Sign post
–*– –Bridge
) – View point
(T)Telephone.

Crich

Food store

Bus

National Tramway Museum

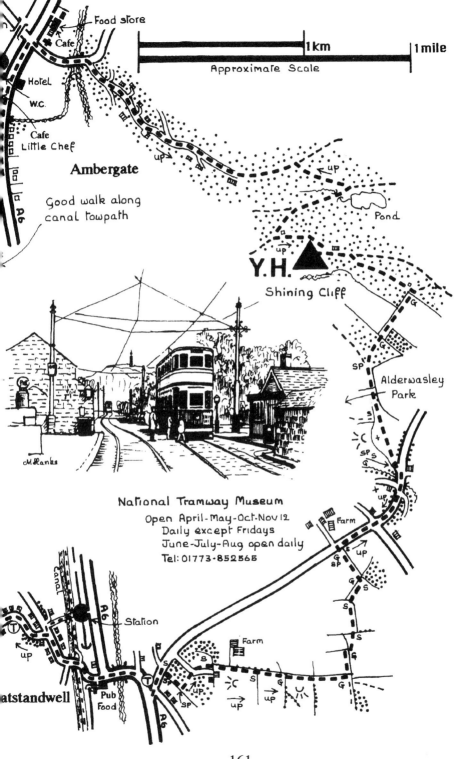

Food store

Cafe

Hotel

W.C.

Cafe
Little Chef

Ambergate

Good walk along
canal towpath

1km   1 mile

Approximate Scale

up

up

Pond

Y.H.

Shining Cliff

Alderwasley
Park

Farm

National Tramway Museum
Open April-May-Oct-Nov 12
Daily except Fridays
June-July-Aug open daily
Tel: 01773-852565

M⁴Ranks

Canal

Station

Farm

up

up

up

atstandwell

Pub
Food

Walks around Crowden

Short walks north of the hostel

(OS Outdoor Leisure Map 1)

Map 65 (see page 164 / 165)   2.5 miles (4km)

Crowden is at the end of the first leg of the Pennine Way, which starts in Edale. This short path joins the Way for a distance, climbing up towards Black Tor above the Crowden Brook. The Way continues northwards to cross Bleaklow (not recommended unless you are properly equipped for walking on exposed moorland). However, a path descends into the valley to cross the brook.

It returns downstream, crossing the tributary Crowden Little Brook to return to the hostel. This may be extended by a walk up to Crowden Quarry and then dropping down to St James's Chapel near Woodhead Reservoir dam. Cross the A628 to reach the path which returns back to the youth hostel by the water channel.

The Longdendale Reservoirs

(OS Outdoor Leisure Map 1)

Around Torside Reservoir 4 miles (6.5km)   To Tintwistle 9.5 miles (15km)

Map 66 (see page 166 / 167)

The five reservoirs in the Longdendale Valley collectively are one of the largest surface areas of man-made water in the country. The closure of the cross-Pennine railway via the Woodhead Tunnel allowed for the creation of the Longdendale Trail between Padfield and the tunnel, east of Crowden. This has in turn created a convenient circular route taking in both sides of the valley.

Proceed down the northside of the valley to Tintwistle (this gives the sun more time to reach the trail). Take the path from the village to cross the Valehouse Reservoir Dam and climb up to the Longdendale Trail. Follow this up past Rhodeswood and Torside Reservoirs. Cross the valley below Woodhead Dam and follow the water channel back to the youth hostel. The trail continues to the far end of Woodhead Reservoir.

Walks around Langsett

(OS Outdoor Leisure Map 1)

Around Langsett Reservoir

4.5 miles (7km)

Map 67 (see page 168 / 169)

Cross the busy A616 and walk around to the dam of the reservoir. The unusual valve tower is modelled on a tower at Lancaster Castle. Cross the dam and follow the road through the wood before turning right to reach Upper Midhope. From here, the path descends through the wood to reach the water before climbing away up onto Hingcliff Common with splendid views across the moors. Much of the Common is open access land. This means that for much of the year, you may wander at will, but it is recommended that you keep to the path.

Near the top of the hill, the path reaches Cut Gate, an old packhorse route to the Derwent Valley, reaching the latter at Slippery Stones, just north of Howden Reservoir. The route to take descends down to Brook House bridge. Return to Langsett through Langsett Bank Woods. There is a National Park Information centre at the village (see map), which is passed on this walk.

Langsett to Midhopestones & Penistone

(OS Outdoor Leisure Map 1)

Map 68 (see page 170 / 171)   6 miles (9.5km)

This route goes down the valley from the youth hostel and then climbs up onto the hill below Penistone, descending back to the youth hostel.

Cross the A616 and walk along the reservoir dam, built between 1889-1904. Turn left at the signpost at the end of the wood and follow the valley of the Little Don River down to Midhopestones. It passes Midhope Reservoir, built to supply water to Barnsley. At Midhopestones, look out for the little church dedicated to St James. It is believed to date from the 1590's. At the Midhopestones Arms, turn left to reach the A616.

Near the bridge is the Potter's Well a reminder of the former Midhope Pottery, built nearby by William Gough. Cross the A616 and go under the former railway bridge. The path climbs up the hill past Judd Field to reach Mossley Road with Penistone village ahead. Turn left along the road which is an old saltway to the Sheffield area from Cheshire. Bear left at the T-junction and after four fields on the left, a path descends back down the hill to Langsett. Either walk into the village or turn right up the field by the hostel to reach the rear of the building. The best view of the hostel for a photograph is from the bottom end of this field!

Walks around Edwinstowe

Edwinstowe to Rufford Abbey

(OS Explorer Series No 28)

Map 69 (see pages 172 / 173)   9 miles (14.5km)

Walk to the crossroads on the A6075 and go straight over to the railway line. Turn left and walk along side the railway until it reaches the A614. Cross the main road and take a path which runs parallel to the A614 to Rufford Abbey & Country Park. If you wish, you can detour on reaching the A614 for about a mile to visit Ollerton Mill. Built in 1713, it is the last working watermill in Nottinghamshire. It is open on Sundays, April-September and Bank Holidays. A tea shop is open March-October excluding Mondays.

At Rufford, there are the remains of the 12th-century Cistercian Abbey. There is a cafe and craft centre here and the Abbey is under the care of English Heritage. Opposite Rufford Abbey on the A614 you will be able to see lots of chalets in a wood. These are part of the Center Parcs Holiday Village. Turn left along the A614. It is a busy road, so keep off the highway. Turn right along a lane and then follow a track which skirts the holiday village perimeter fence. Then cross fields and the railway to reach the River Maun.

The path follows the river upstream before turning right past Archway House to reach the A6075. Turn right here and then left to return through the wood to the youth hostel.

Edwinstowe to The Major Oak

Map 70 (see pages 174 / 175)

This is a short walk of about thirty minutes to visit the Major Oak. This is believed to be about 800 years old and traditionally is associated with Robin Hood. Walk past the cricket ground and childrens' play area to the Visitor Centre and the Sherwood Forest Exhibition. A well defined path goes on to the Major Oak. Note the alternative path back to the youth hostel shown on the map.

Touring from Sherwood Forest YH

Map 71 (see page 176 / 177)   26 miles (41 km)

Indicates a recommended cycle route on quiet lanes and tracks which takes in Sherwood Forest, Holbeck village, Creswell Crags. where Ice Age hunters lived ,and then on to Clumber Park, where the National Trust has its regional office. There is a visitor centre, cafe and cycle hire facility here.

If you have arrived by car, there are numerous country houses in the district. In fact it is known as The Dukeries, so many aristocratic families lived in this area. Within twenty miles or so may be visited: Rufford Abbey: (English Heritage/Notts City Council); Clumber Park: (National Trust); Hardwick Hall: (National Trust); Bolsover Castle: (English Heritage); Sutton Scarsdale Hall: (English Heritage) and Newstead Abbey.

A little further north are Roche Abbey: (English Heritage); Oddsock Priory, famous for its snowdrops; and the ruined Mattersey Priory (English Heritage).

South west of Old Clipstone and on the B6030, is the Sherwood Pines Visitor Centre, run by Forest Enterprise (the Forestry Commission). There are waymarked walks, cycle routes and a cycle hire centre, cafe and shop. It is open daily except for Christmas Day.

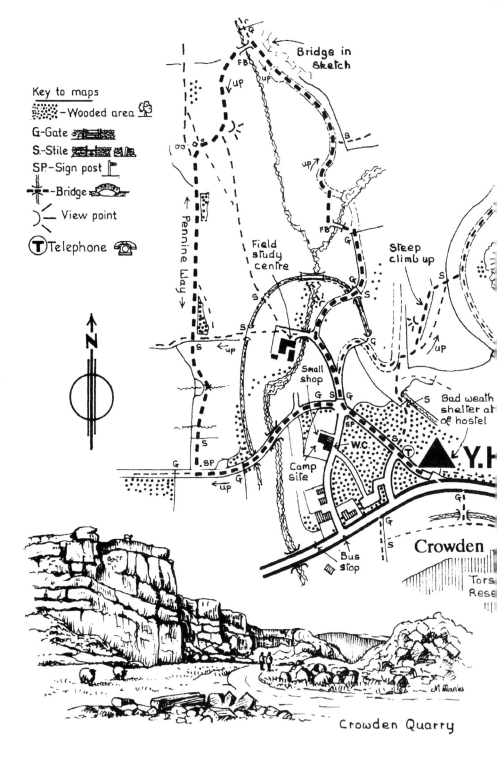

Key to maps
▦ – Wooded area 🌳
G – Gate
S. – Stile
SP – Sign post
–‡– Bridge
View point
Ⓣ Telephone ☎

N

Bridge in Sketch

FB
up
up
c
G

up

S

up↗

Pennine Way

Field study centre

FB
G

G
S

Steep climb up

S

up

S

Small shop

G S G

G

s Bad weather shelter at of hostel

SP
S T
W.C.
Ⓣ
▲ Y.H

Camp site

G
SP
S
G

up

G
S

Bus stop

Crowden

G

S

Tors Rese

Crowden Quarry

M Davies

164

Map 65
Walks around Crowden
see page 162

Track poor

390m
1250ft

Crowden
Quarry

up
S G
up

Quarry not
recommended for
rock climbing

St James's
Chapel

up
G

628
G

Woodhead
Reservoir

B6105

Crowden Youth Hostel
Tel: 01457-852135

Short walk 2.5miles 4 km
- - - -

Manchester-Sheffield buse
serve Crowden 5 times a day
each way.

Bridge on short walk

M Banks 98

Map 66
Walks around Longdendale Reservoirs
Torside Reservoir to Tintwistle

see page 162

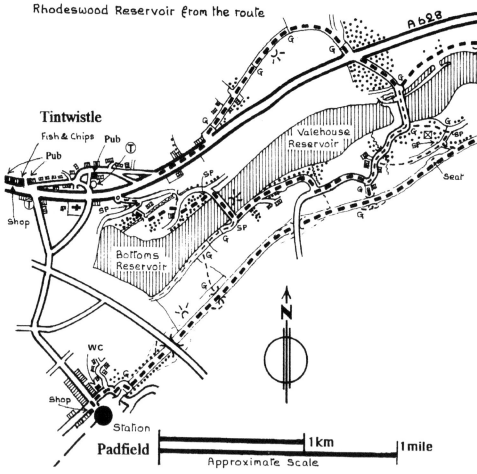

Rhodeswood Reservoir from the route

Tintwistle

Fish & Chips Pub

Pub

Shop

Valehouse Reservoir

Seat

Bottoms Reservoir

N

WC

Shop

Station

Padfield

A628

1km

1mile

Approximate Scale

Approximate distance of main circular route
to Tintwistle 9.5miles 15 km ▪ ▪ ▪ ▪

Distance round Torside Reservoir 4miles 6.5 km

Distance by shortest route to Padfield
4.75mile 7.5 km

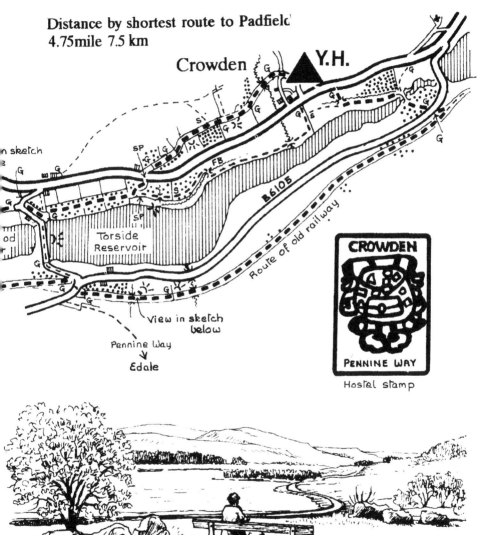

Crowden Y.H.

Torside
Reservoir

B6105

Route of old railway

View in sketch
below

Pennine Way
↓
Edale

CROWDEN

PENNINE WAY

Hostel stamp

View over Torside Reservoir

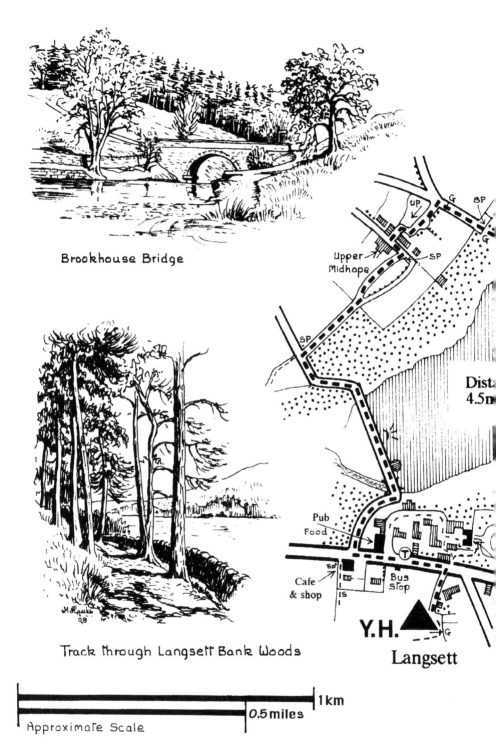

Brookhouse Bridge

Track through Langsett Bank Woods

Upper Midhope

Dist...
4.5m

Pub Food

Cafe & shop

Bus Stop

Y.H.

Langsett

1km
0.5 miles
Approximate Scale

Map 67
Walk around Langsett Reservoir
see page 162

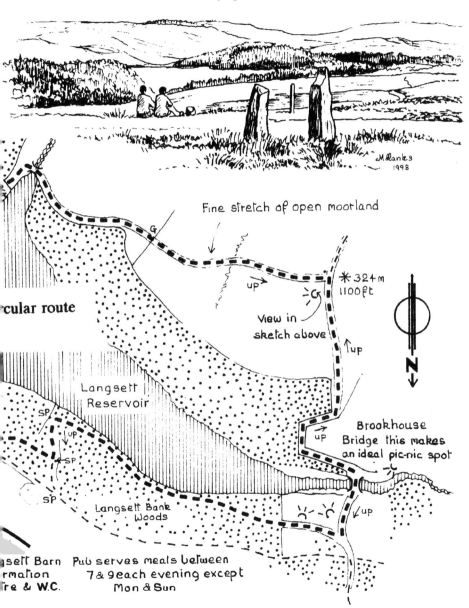

M.Dankes 1998

Fine stretch of open moorland

G

circular route

UP

✳ 324 m
1100 ft

View in
sketch above

↑ up

Langsett
Reservoir

SP

↑ up

SP

Brookhouse
Bridge this makes
an ideal pic-nic spot

N

↓ up

SP

Langsett Bank
Woods

↓ up

Langsett Barn
rmation
re & W.C.

Pub serves meals between
7 & 9 each evening except
Mon & Sun

Map 68
Langsett to Midhopestones & Penistone
see page 162

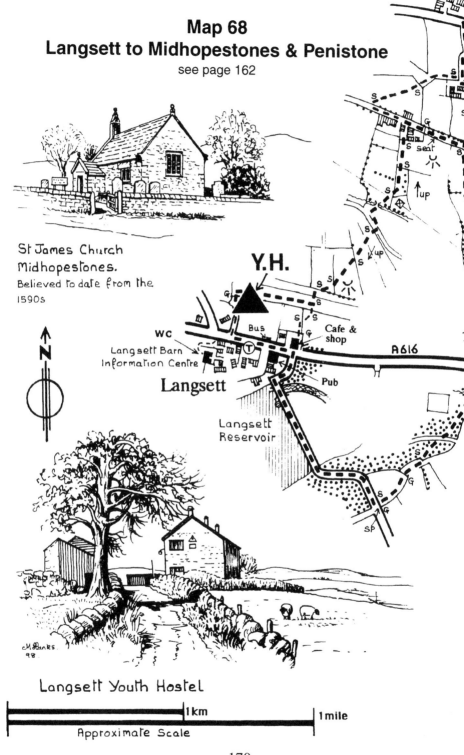

St James Church Midhopestones. Believed to date from the 1590s

Y.H.

WC

Langsett Barn Information Centre

Bus

Cafe & shop

A616

Langsett

Pub

N

Langsett Reservoir

Langsett Youth Hostel

| 1km | 1mile |

Approximate Scale

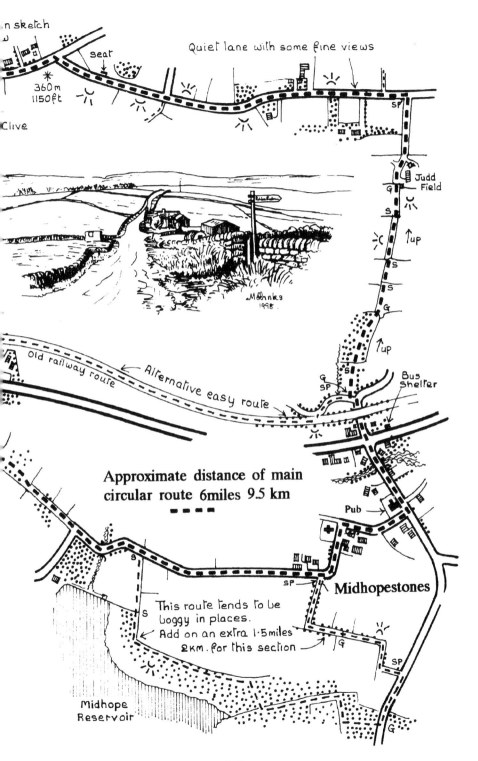

n sketch

seat

Quiet lane with some fine views

360m
1150ft

Clive

SP

Judd Field

G

S

↑up

S

S

G

↑up

Old railway route

Alternative easy route

G
SP

S

Bus Shelter

Approximate distance of main circular route 6 miles 9.5 km

- - - -

Pub

S

Midhopestones

SP

This route tends to be boggy in places.
Add on an extra 1·5 miles 2km. for this section

S

G

SP

Midhope Reservoir

G

M Monks 1998

Map 69
Edwinstowe to Rufford Abbey
see page 163

Approximate distance of main circular
route 9miles 14.5 km - - - -

1km 1mile

Approximate Scale

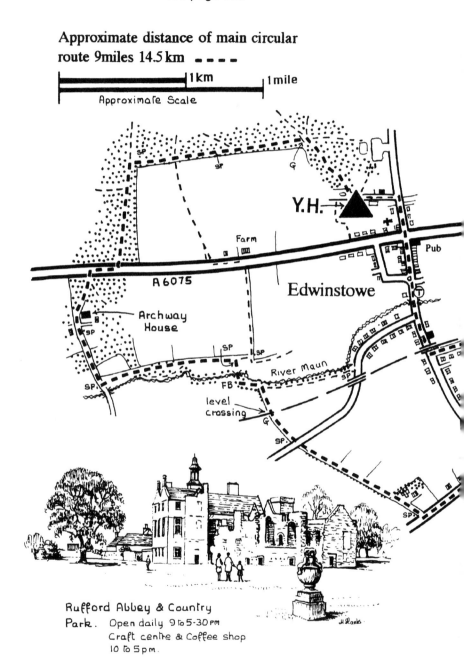

A 6075

Y.H.

Farm

Pub

Edwinstowe

Archway
House

River Maun

FB

level
crossing

Rufford Abbey & Country
Park. Open daily 9 to 5:30 pm
Craft centre & Coffee shop
10 to 5 pm.

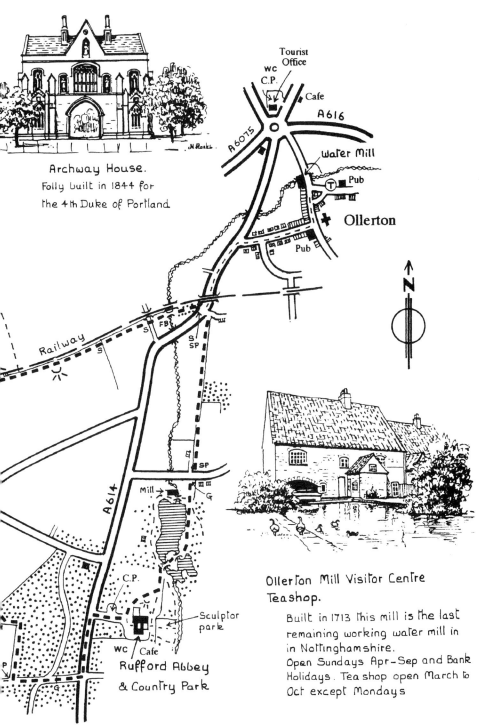

Archway House.
Folly built in 1844 for
the 4th Duke of Portland

Tourist
Office
wc
C.P.
Cafe
A616
A6075
water Mill
Pub
Ollerton
Pub
Railway
S
FB
S
SP
N
SP
A614
Mill
G
SP
C.P.
Sculptor
park
wc Cafe
**Rufford Abbey
& Country Park**
P
G

**Ollerton Mill Visitor Centre
Teashop.**

Built in 1713 this mill is the last
remaining working water mill in
in Nottinghamshire.
Open Sundays Apr-Sep and Bank
Holidays. Tea shop open March to
Oct except Mondays

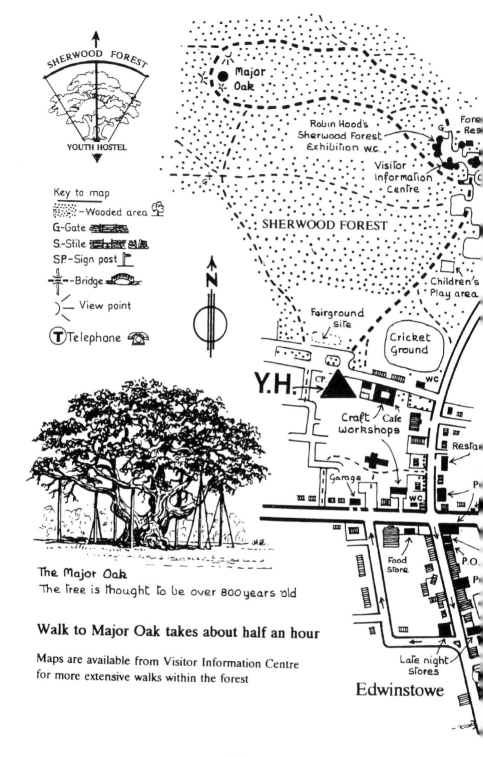

SHERWOOD FOREST

YOUTH HOSTEL

Key to map

- ░ – Wooded area
- G – Gate
- S. – Stile
- SP. – Sign post
- –†– – Bridge
-)– – View point
- (T) Telephone

N

Major Oak

Robin Hood's Sherwood Forest Exhibition W.C.

Fore Res

Visitor Information Centre

SHERWOOD FOREST

Children's Play area

Fairground site

Cricket Ground

Y.H.

C.P.

WC

Craft workshops

Cafe

Resta

Garage

WC.

P

Food Store

P.O.

P

Late night stores

Edwinstowe

The Major Oak

The tree is thought to be over 800 years old

Walk to Major Oak takes about half an hour

Maps are available from Visitor Information Centre for more extensive walks within the forest

Map 70
Edwinstowe to Major Oak
see page 163

Sherwood Forest Youth Hostel

Tel: 01623 825794

stop
gular buses to Mansfield
ksop & Nottingham

The cricket ground Edwinstowe

Designed by M Hanks.

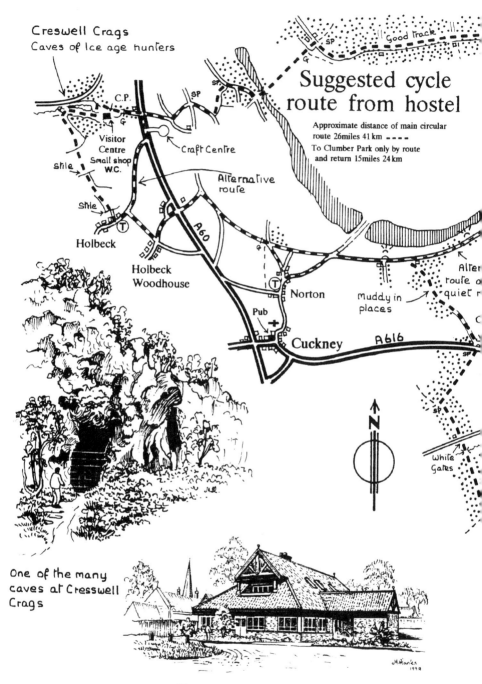

Creswell Crags
Caves of Ice age hunters

Good track

SP

Suggested cycle route from hostel

Approximate distance of main circular
route 26miles 41 km - - - -
To Clumber Park only by route
and return 15miles 24 km

C.P.

SP

Visitor
Centre
Small shop
W.C.

Craft Centre

stile

Alternative
route

stile

(T)

Holbeck

A60

**Holbeck
Woodhouse**

Alter
route a
quiet r

Norton

muddy in
places

C

Pub

Cuckney   A616

White
Gates

N

One of the many
caves at Cresswell
Crags

M. Manley
1998

Sherwood Forest Youth Hostel
Tel: 01623 825794

176

Map 71
Touring from
Sherwood Forest
see page 163

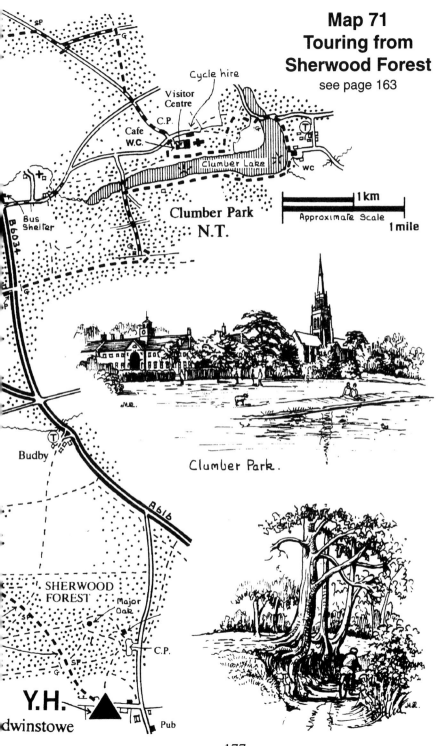

Cycle hire

Visitor
Centre

C.P.

Cafe
W.C.

Clumber Lake

wc

Clumber Park
N.T.

1 km
Approximate Scale
1 mile

Bus
Shelter

B6034

Clumber Park.

Budby

A616

SHERWOOD
FOREST

Major
Oak

C.P.

Y.H.
dwinstowe

Pub

SP

177

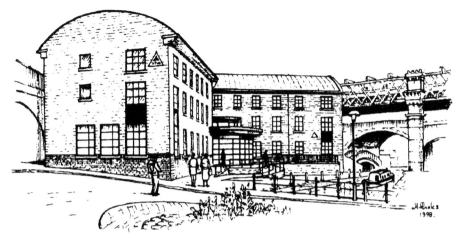

Manchester Youth Hostel
Tel: 0161-839 9960

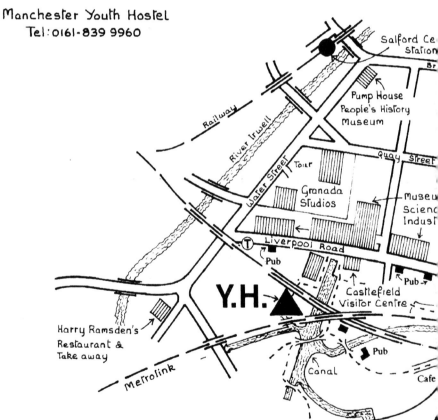

Salford Ce
Station

Pump House
People's History
Museum

Railway

River Irwell

Water Street

Tour

Quay Street

Granada
Studios

Museu
Scienc
Indust

Liverpool Road

Pub

Y.H.

Castlefield
Visitor Centre

Pub

Harry Ramsden's
Restaurant &
Take away

Metrolink

Canal

Pub

Cafe

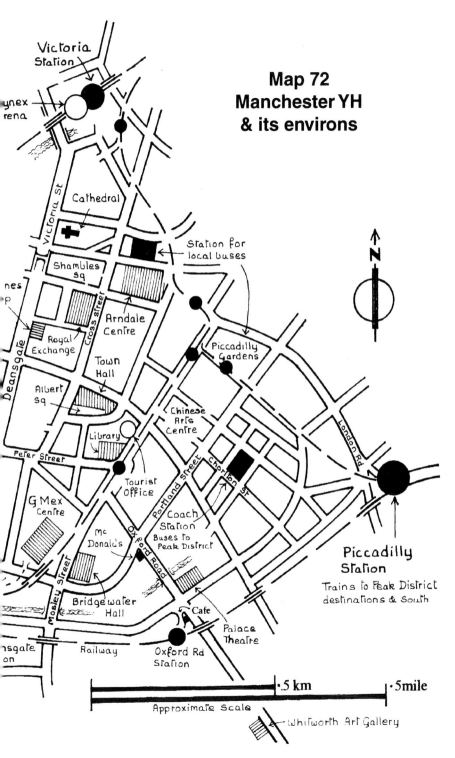

Map 72
Manchester YH
& its environs

Victoria Station

ynex rena

Victoria St

Cathedral

Station for local buses

Shambles sq

nes
P

Cross Street

Arndale Centre

Royal Exchange

Deansgate

Town Hall

Piccadilly Gardens

Albert sq

Library

Chinese Arts Centre

London Rd

Peter Street

Tourist Office

Portland Street

Chorlton St

G Mex Centre

mc Donald's

Oxford Road

Coach Station
Buses to Peak District

Piccadilly Station
Trains to Peak District destinations & South

Mosley Street

Bridgewater Hall

Cafe

Palace Theatre

nsgate on

Railway

Oxford Rd Station

·5 km

·5 mile

Approximate Scale

Whitworth Art Gallery

179

THE YOUTH HOSTELS

Opening dates, days and times in this book relate to 1998. Please note that subsequent years may vary a little.

Bakewell YH

Fly Hill, Bakewell, Derbyshire DE45 1DN
☎/Fax: 01629 812313

Accommodation details:

A modern building with 36 beds. Two 6 and two 12 bedded rooms. Access during the day. Wet weather shelter/luggage store and cycle store.

Other facilities include: lounge, drying room, self-catering kitchen, showers and small shop. Dinner served 19.00.

Open: 2 January to 26 March Friday, Saturday; 27 March to 14 June except Sunday*; daily 15 June to 30 August daily; 31 August to 31 October except Sunday*; 1 November to 23 December Friday, Saturday; 24-26 December.

Advance bookings may be accepted when closed.

*Open Bank Holiday Sunday/Closed Bank Holiday Monday.

Getting there:

By bus: Frequent buses from surrounding areas. ☎ 01332 292200.

By rail: Matlock 8m (12.8km).

Description:

Near the town centre, this small youth hostel is built in the grounds of Bagshaw Hall. Small car park — parking in town centre. Bakewell is at the heart of the National Park and its shops and Monday market attract many visitors. There are excellent walks in limestone dales and along gritstone edges, and Bakewell is on the popular White Peak Way. Nearby are Chatsworth House and Haddon Hall.

Bretton YH

Nr Eyam
Bookings: c/o John and Elaine Whittington, 7 New Bailey, Crane Moor, Sheffield S35 7AT
☎ 0114 2884541

Accommodation details:

This hostel has one room each of 4, 6 and 8 beds. Other facilities include: lounge/dining room, self-catering kitchen, shower, drying room, cycle store and grounds. No shop. Self catering only.

Open: 1 January to 31 July Friday, Saturday, Bank Holiday Sundays; daily 1-31 August; 1 September to 19 December Friday, Saturday.

Advance bookings may be accepted when closed. Rent-a-Hostel available 1 January to 28 March; 2 November to 31 December; Sunday to Thursday.

Please note, hostel opens at 19.30 on Fridays.

Getting there:

Situated 1.5m (2.4km) NW of Eyam, behind Barrel Inn on Great Hucklow-Grindleford Road.

By bus: Services from Sheffield, Buxton and Chesterfield (passing close to station) alight Foolow, 1m. ☎ 01298 23098.

By rail: Sheffield, Buxton and Chesterfield. Grindleford 4m (6.4km); Hathersage 4m (6.4km).

Description:

Rebuilt in the 1970s, a small, simple hostel situated 1250ft (385m) high on Eyam Edge enjoying superb views across unspoilt countryside. Less than two miles from the historic plague village of Eyam, with its fascinating church and monuments. Run by dedicated volunteers, it has a wonderful atmosphere.

Buxton YH

Sherbrook Lodge, Harpur Hill Road, Buxton, Derbyshire SK17 9NB
☎/Fax: 01298 22287

Accommodation details:

This Victorian house in wooded grounds has mostly 4-8 bedded rooms plus one 10 and one

12 bedded room. Access during the day. Cycle store and wet weather shelter. Other facilities include: lounge, self-catering kitchen, dining room, showers, drying room and luggage store. Evening meal served 19.00.

Open: 6 February to 27 March Friday, Saturday; 28 March to 13 December except Sunday*; 24-26 December special package please enquire.

Advance bookings accepted when closed.

*Open Bank Holiday Sundays, closed Bank Holiday Mondays.

Getting there:

3/4m (1.2km) south of Market Place on junction between A515 Ashbourne Road and Harpur Hill Road.

By bus: Frequent from surrounding areas. Different operators. ☎ 01298 23098. On the route of the TP Trans Peak bus between Manchester and Nottingham.

By rail: Buxton 1.5m (2.4km).

Description:

A detached former quarry manager's house in extensive grounds, about a mile from the town centre. Situated on the edge of the Peak National Park, Buxton has all the attractions of a busy spa town within walking distance. There are some fine buildings, shops and an indoor swimming pool. Local attractions include Alton Towers and Chatsworth House.

Castleton YH

Castleton Hall, Castleton, Hope Valley S33 8WG
☎ 01433 620235 Fax: 01433 621767

Accommodation details:

Situated in the heart of Castleton village, this hostel has 150 beds. The rooms are 2, 4, and 6 bedded plus one 16 bedded room. Facilities: lounges, TV room, games rooms, self-catering kitchen, showers, drying room, cycle shed and luggage store. Evening meal served between 18.00-19.00. Table licence.

Open: daily 6 February to 23 December; 24 December to 5 February Rent-a-Hostel.

Getting there:

A625 from Sheffield, once in village, turn left into Market Place. A625 from Manchester, then Winnats Pass.

By bus: Mainline/Stagecoach East Midland 272/4 from Sheffield (passes Hope station). ☎ 01298 23098.

By rail: Hope 3m (4.8km).

Description:

18th century Castleton Hall and the adjacent 19th century Old Vicarage are situated in the village square. In 1996 YHA opened eight ensuite rooms in the adjacent former vicarage, together with two larger suites of rooms in a barn conversion at the rear. The Hall has been recently refurbished. Local attractions include Treak Cliff Cavern, Blue John Mine, Speedwell Cavern and Peak Cavern. The ruins of Peveril Castle are just above the hostel.

Crowden-in-Longdendale YH

Peak National Park Hostel, Crowden, Hadfield, Hyde, Cheshire SK14 7HZ
☎/Fax: 01457 852135

Accommodation details:

This traditional hostel has 50 beds. Several 2-4 bedded, one each 6 and 8 and two 12 bedded rooms. Access during the day. Wet weather shelter. Other facilities include: lounge, self-catering kitchen, showers, drying room and cycle store. Evening meal served 19.30.

Open: 1 January to 5 March Rent-a-Hostel; 6-26 March Friday, Saturday; 27 March to 2 May except Wednesday; daily 3 May to 31 October; 1-28 November Friday, Saturday; 29 November to 30 December Rent-a-Hostel; 31 December to 2 January.

Advance bookings accepted when closed.

Getting there:

On north side of Manchester - Barnsley Road (A628) marked 'Crowden' on map.

By bus: National Express Sheffield-Manchester (passes close Sheffield station), 350 service.

By rail: Hadfield (not Sunday) 5m (8km).

Description:

Overlooking the reservoirs of the Longdendale valley, this traditional hostel with basic amenities was converted from a row of railwayman's cottages. On the Pennine Way, it is surrounded by high level walking country. Popular with walkers and climbers exploring the remote moorlands of the northern Peak District. A convenient rural base for Manchester.

Dimmingsdale YH

Little Ranger, Dimmingsdale, Oakamoor, Stoke on Trent, Staffordshire ST10 3AS
☎ 01538 702304

Accommodation details:

This simple hostel has 20 beds, two 6 and one 8 bedded rooms. Other facilities include: common room, self-catering kitchen, shower, drying room and cycle store. Limited shop. Self-catering only.

Open: 1 January to 26 March Rent-a- Hostel; 27 March to 31 May except Sunday*; daily 1 June to 30 August; 31 August to 31 October except Sunday; 1 November to 28 February Rent-a-Hostel.

Advance bookings accepted when closed.

*Open Bank Holiday Sunday, closed Bank Holiday Monday.

Getting there:

From Oakamoor off B5417, take road at the south end of bridge past Admiral Jervis. Take right fork to top of hill, turn left up farm track to hostel.

By bus: PMT 238 from Uttoxeter (passes close to station), alight Oakamoor, 3/4m (1.2km). ☎ 01785 223344.

By rail: Blythe Bridge 6m (9.6km).

Description:

A small, simple hostel in secluded woodland near several nature reserves, the Caldon Canal and the valleys of Dimmingsdale and the Churnet. Ideally situated in some good walking country and less used than the main area of the Peak. Two miles from Alton Towers Theme Park and close to pottery museums at Stoke on Trent.

Edale YH

Rowland Cote, Nether Booth, Edale, Hope Valley S33 7ZH
☎ 01433 670302 Fax: 01433 670243

Accommodation details:

Situated in the lovely Edale Valley, this hostel has 141 beds. Mostly 6-8 bedded plus two 12 bedded rooms. Access during the day, lounge, games room with TV, self-catering kitchen, showers, drying room, cycle store, laundry, grounds and hot & cold drinks. Other facilities include outdoor activities (book in advance). Evening meal served between 17.30 and 19.15. Table licence.

Open: daily 1 January to 23 December; 24 December to 2 January (special event, please enquire).

Getting there:

1 mile (1.6km) east of Edale village marked 'Rowland Cote' on OS. Good road and rail access.

No bus service.

By rail: Edale 2m (3.2km). On Friday evenings (16.00-20.00), all trains are met to take you to the hostel.

Description:

A large hostel situated at Nether Booth, a couple of miles from Edale village and just below the Kinder Scout moors. The house was originally the home of the Batchelor family — better known for their peas.

Ideally placed as an activity centre, at certain times of year it may not be appropriate to use this hostel for other purposes. Check with the hostel and, if necessary, use nearby Castleton YH or Hathersage YH instead. Edale is the start of the Pennine Way.

Elton YH

Elton Old Hall, Main Street, Elton, Matlock, Derbyshire DE4 2BW
☎ 01629 650394

Accommodation details:

This hostel has 32 beds. Two 4, one each 6, 8 and 10 bedded rooms. Access during the day, luggage storage, lounge, self-catering kitchen, shower, drying room and cycle store. Limited snack meals service: continental breakfasts, evening snacks and packed lunches.

Open: daily 13 February to 31 October; 27 December to 2 January.

Advance bookings may be accepted when closed.

Getting there:

The hostel is at the east end of Elton village on Main Street.

By bus: Hulleys 170 Matlock-Bakewell (passes close Matlock station) ☎ 01298 23098.

By rail: Matlock 5m (8km).

Description:

A 17th century listed building on the main street of the village. This is a small, simple hostel housed in the Old Hall. It is close to the market towns of Matlock and Bakewell. Chatsworth House and Haddon Hall are within easy reach.

Eyam YH

Hawkhill Road, Eyam, Hope Valley S32 5QX
☎/Fax: 01433 630335

Accommodation details:

This Victorian house has 60 beds. Several 2-4 bedded, mostly 8 bedded plus two 10 bedded rooms. Access during day, toilet and luggage store. Other facilities include: lounge, games room, self-catering kitchen, drying room and cycle store. Evening meal served at 18.30.

Open: 6-28 February Friday, Saturday; 1-30 March except Sunday; daily 1 April to 30 September; 1-31 October except Sunday; 1-28

November open Friday, Saturday; 27 December to 3 January.

Advance bookings accepted when closed.

Getting there:

Follow signs to the public/coach park and continue up the hill — hostel 600yds on the left past 'The Edge' and 'Windward House'.

By bus: Various services from Sheffield, Buxton & Chesterfield (passing close Sheffield, Buxton, Chesterfield stations), alight Foolow, 1m (1.6km) ☎ 01298 23098.

By rail: Grindleford 3.5m (5.6km); Hathersage 4m (6.4km).

Description:

A Victorian house perched on a wooded hillside overlooking the village (infected by the Great Plague of London 1665). This hostel is currently being upgraded with the aim of providing more family sized rooms. It is an ideal base for exploring the Peak District and Eyam Hall, Chatsworth and Haddon Hall. Situated in ideal walking countryside.

Gradbach Mill YH

Gradbach, Quarnford, Buxton, Derbyshire SK17 0SU
☎: 01260 227625 Fax: 01260 227334

Accommodation details:

This former mill has 97 beds. Three 2, one each 3, 8, 10 and seven 4 and 6 bedded rooms. Ground floor suitable for people with disabilities. Access during the day. From 13.00 lounge, self-catering kitchen, showers, drying room, cycle store, luggage store, laundry facilities and grounds. Evening meal served 19.00.

Open: 1-3 January; daily 6 February to 5 December.

Advance bookings accepted when closed.

Getting there:

Hostel clearly signposted from Flash village.

By bus: PMT X23 Sheffield-Hanley (passes close Sheffield & Buxton station), alight Flash Bar Stores, 2.5m (4km). ☎: 01298 23098.

By rail: Buxton 7m (11.2km); Macclesfield 9m (14.4km).

Description:

An old silk mill on the banks of the River Dane in a quiet, unspoilt corner of the Peak District. It is popular with walkers and mountain bikers. The spa town of Buxton with its shops, swimming pool and theatre is just 6m (9.6km) away. Also within easy reach are Alton Towers 14m (22.4km) and the National Trust's Quarry Bank Mill at Styal 20m (32km).

Hartington Hall YH

Hartington, Buxton, Derbyshire SK17 0AT
☎ 01298 84223 Fax: 01298 84415

Accommodation details:

This hostel has 138 beds. One 2, thirteen 4, one 8 and six larger dormitories. Access during the day to all facilities including: reception, bedrooms, dining rooms, lounges, self-catering facilities, drying room, TV room, shop, toilets and showers, laundry, cycle store and games room. Evening meal served between 18.00 and 19.00. Table licence.

Open: daily 13 February to 23 December; 24 December to 2 January (special events, please enquire).

Advance bookings may be accepted when closed.

Getting there:

From centre of village, turn up the lane by the school. The hostel is 200yds up the hill on left.

By bus: Bowers 442 from Buxton station; also from other areas on Sunday and Bank Holidays only. ☎ 01298 23098.

By rail: Buxton 12m (19.2km); Matlock 13m (20.8km).

Description:

Partly dating from the 17th century. Recently refurbished and situated above this attractive village close to the northern entrance to Dovedale. Also convenient distance from Alton Towers, Chatsworth House and Tissington/High Peak Trails for cycle rides. In a rear courtyard are a suite of family rooms situated in a former barn, some ensuite.

Hathersage YH

Castleton Road, Hathersage, Hope Valley, Derbyshire S32 1EH
☎/Fax: 01433 650493

Accommodation details:

This Victorian house has 42 beds. Three 4 and five 6 bedded rooms. Access during the day, drying room, lounge, self-catering kitchen, showers, dining room, cycle store and grounds. Evening meal served at 19.00.

Open: 2 January to 7 April Friday, Saturday; 8 April to 31 October except Sunday*; 1-28 November Friday, Saturday; 31 December to 2 January.

Advance bookings accepted when closed. *Open Bank Holiday Sunday, closed Bank Holiday Monday.

Getting there:

The hostel is 100yds on right past the George Hotel on the road to Castleton.

By bus: Mainline/Stagecoach East Midland 272/4 from Sheffield ☎ 01298 23098.

By rail: Hathersage 0.5m (8km).

Description:

A former villa-type house close to the village centre, with an additional range in an adjacent former barn. This is a good starting point for exploring the Peak District and the White Peak Way circular walk. Sheffield is 10m (16km).

Ilam YH

Ilam Hall, Ashbourne, Derbyshire DE6 2AZ
☎ 01335 350212 Fax: 01335 350350

Accommodation details:

This hostel has 148 beds, mostly 3-8 bedded plus one 13 and one 16 bedded room. Access during the day, lounge, TV room, games room, self- catering kitchen, showers, drying room, cycle store, laundry facilities and grounds. Evening meal served between 18.00 and 20.00. Table licence.

Open: daily 1 February to 31 October; 1-30

November Friday, Saturday; 30 December to 1 January (special event, please enquire).

Advance bookings accepted when closed.

Getting there:

From Ilam village centre, enter the National Trust Country Park and follow drive to the Hall.

By bus: Infrequent from Ashbourne; otherwise from Derby, Manchester (passing close Derby & Macclesfield stations), alight Ilam Cross Roads 2.5m (4km), or Ashbourne 6m (9.6km) for bus, taxi ☎ 01332 292200.

By rail: Matlock 20m (32km); Uttoxeter 15m (24km); Derby 18m (28.8km).

Description:

This hostel was recently refurbished, providing a lot of small family sized rooms. Two rooms suitable for wheelchair users. Situated in a beautiful area, close to Dovedale. Alton Towers is only 9m (14.4km) away. It is part of a much larger Tudor Gothic house demolished in 1935.

Splendid situation, with large grounds which are now a country park.

Langsett YH

Langsett village, near Penistone. Bookings to: c/o J & E Whittington, 7 New Bailey, Crane Moor, Sheffield S35 7AT
☎ 0114 2884541

Accommodation details:

This hostel has 34 beds. Four 4, one 8 and one 10 bedded rooms. Access during the day: porch and toilet. Other facilities: lounge/dining room, two self-catering kitchens, shower, drying room, cycle store and garden. Credit cards accepted for advance bookings only. No shop. Self-catering only.

Open: 1 January to 17 July Friday, Saturday, Bank Holiday Sunday; daily 18 July to 30 August; 31 August to 19 December Friday, Saturday. Hostel open from 19.30 on Friday.

Getting there:

100yds up the track just of the A616 1m (1.6km)

south-east of Flouch roundabout.

By bus: Barnsley & District/Yorkshire Traction 381 from Barnsley station (passes close Penistone station) ☎ 01709 515151.

By rail: Penistone 3m (4.8km).

Description:

Built as a youth hostel about thirty years ago, this is a small and cosy simple grade building.

Matlock YH

40 Bank Road, Matlock, Derbyshire DE4 3NF
☎ 01629 582983 Fax: 01629 583484

Accommodation details

This 49 bedded hostel has four 2, two 3, five 4, one 6 and one 9 bedded rooms. Access during the day from 13.00. Lounge, TV room, games room, self-catering kitchen, showers, drying room, cycle store, laundry facilities, grounds, training and conference rooms. Evening meal served at 19.00. Table licence.

Open: daily 1 January to 23 December; 24-26 December (special event, please enquire).

From Crown Square, the hostel is 200yds up Bank Road on right.

By bus: Frequent from surrounding areas ☎ 01332 292200.

By rail: Matlock 400yds.

Description:

This former cottage hospital opened as a youth hostel in 1984. It has several small family rooms. There is a cinema and swimming pool in the town. The National Tramway Museum, cable cars and American Adventure Theme Park are close by.

Meerbrook YH

Old School, Meerbrook, Leek, Staffordshire ST13 8SJ
Bookings c/o: Mrs E Nettel, Cornerhouse, Roache Road, Upperhulme, Nr Leek ST13 8UQ.
☎ 01538 300148

Accommodation details:

This basic hostel has 22 beds, two 2, one 8 and one 10 bedded room. Facilities include: lounge, self-catering kitchen, shower, drying room, cycle store and grounds. No shop. Credit cards accepted for advance bookings only. Self-catering only.

Open: 1 January to 2 April Rent-a-Hostel; 3 April to 4 July Friday, Saturday*/**; daily 5 July to 12 September; 13 September to 31 October Friday, Saturday*; 1 November to 28 February Rent-a-Hostel.

* Open Bank Holiday Sunday. ** Rent-a-Hostel Sunday to Thursday (except on Bank Holiday Sunday).

Getting there:

From A53 Buxton-Leek road, take turning by Three Horseshoes public house, signposted Meerbrook. Follow road past Tittesworth reservoir into centre of village. Hostel is on right hand side, past the pub.

By bus: PMT X23 Sheffield-Hanley (passes close Stoke-on-Trent & Buxton stations), alight Blackshaw Moor, 2m (3.2km) ☎ 01298 23098.

By rail: Stoke-on-Trent 15m (24km).

Description:

This hostel popular, with walkers and groups, is situated in a quiet corner of the Staffordshire Moorlands. The Roaches (for climbing) and Staffordshire's museums, factory shops and potteries are nearby. It used to be the village school.

Ravenstor YH

Millers Dale, Buxton, Derbyshire SK17 8SS
☎ 01298 871826 Fax: 01298 871275

Accommodation details:

This 82 bedded hostel has one each 2, 3, 4, 7, 8, 10, 12, 16 and 20 bedded room. Access during the day. Open from 13.00. Reception, lounge, dining room, TV room/study, self-catering kitchen, showers and cycle store. Evening meal served at 19.00. Table licence.

Open: 1-3 January; 6 February to 31 March except Sunday; daily 1 April to 31 October; 1 November to 19 December Friday, Saturday.

Advance bookings accepted when closed.

Getting there:

From A6 between Bakewell and Buxton, take the B6049 to Tideswell. The hostel is 1m (1.6km) past Millers Dale.

By bus: From Sheffield, Buxton (passes close to Sheffield & Buxton stations)
☎ 01298 23098.

By rail: Buxton 8m (12.8km).

Description:

A large country house situated on the River Wye in Millers Dale, between Buxton and Bakewell. A lovely, recently refurbished youth hostel in an incomparable location.

Sherwood Forest YH

Forest Corner, Edwinstowe, Nottinghamshire NG21
☎ 01623 825794 Fax: 01623 825796

Accommodation Details

This new, purpose-built hostel has 46 beds, all in small rooms. Access from 13.00 to all facilities: lounge, bedrooms, toilets, drying room, self-catering kitchen and cycle store. Facilities for people with disabilities. Evening meal served at 19.00. Open every day.

Getting there:

Approach from B6034. From Edwinstowe/south take the first turning on the left after traffic lights. From the north take 1st turning on right after Visitor Centre.

By bus: Stagecoach 33 or 36 from Nottingham.

By rail: Mansfield Woodhouse 5m (8km) (Robin Hood line from Nottingham)

Description:

A brand new hostel opened in 1998 close to the Sherwood Forest Visitor Centre (with Robin Hood's Major Oak). Family sized rooms.

Manchester YH

Potato Wharf, Castlefield, Gtr Manchester M3 4NB
℅ 0161 839 9960 Fax: 0161 835 2054

Accommodation Details

This new youth hostel has 152 beds. All are in small ensuite rooms. Open all day (but access to bedrooms restricted at certain times during the day). Cafeteria service between 17.30-19.45hrs. Table licence. **Open:** daily.

Getting there:

From Piccadilly train station and the bus station, it is a pleasant stroll through the city centre; follow signs for Castlefield/Museum of Science and Industry (MSI).

By bus: Number 33 from Piccadilly Gardens (℅ 0161 228 7811)

By tram: Take the GM Metrolink to G-Mex which is a few minutes away

By train: Deansgate Station (see map, page)

page)

By car: Follow signs for Castlefields/MSI. The youth hostel is behind the Castlefield Hotel and opposite the MSI.

Description:

Manchester Youth Hostel is established in historic Castlefields. This was Britain's first urban heritage park.

Here are the wharfs of the Bridgwater Canal — Britain's first canal. One of the world's first commercial railways (to Liverpool) started from here too. Today, the impressive massive cast iron railway arches still span the canal wharfs with their picturesque narrow boats. Footpaths allow you to explore the waterways and many of the old buildings have been renovated.

Within a short distance of the youth hostel, you can visit the Museum of Science & Industry and Grenada Studios, where 'Coronation Street' is recorded. The Opera House, G-Mex Centre and Bridgwater Hall are also nearby.

The area has cafe bars; towpath trails and narrowboat trips starting from adjacent to the youth hostel. The open air Outdoor Events Arena is next door with events staged throughout the summer.

Castlefields is a vibrant and interesting area to visit as well as being adjacent to the Peak District National Park.

The attractive village of Hollinsclough

LANDMARK
Publishing Ltd ● ● ● ●

VISITORS GUIDES

* Practical guides for the independent traveller

* Written in the form of touring itineraries

* Full colour illustrations and maps

* Detailed Landmark FactFile of practical information

* Landmark Visitors Guides highlight all the interesting places you
  will want to see, so ensuring that you make the most of your visit

1. **Britain**
   Cornwall   Cotswolds &
   Jersey   Shakespeare Country
   Devon   Lake District
   Guernsey   Dorset
   Scotland   Yorkshire Dales & York
   Hampshire   Peak District
   Edinburgh

2. **Europe**
   Bruges   Tuscany
   Provence   Gran Canaria
   Italian Lakes   Lanzerote

3. **Other**
   Dominican Republic   Florida Keys
   India: Goa   Florida: Gulf Coast
   India: Kerala &   Florida: Atlantic Coast
      The South   Orlando & Central Florida
   Gambia   New Zealand

Landmark Publishing
Waterloo House, 12 Compton, Ashbourne, Derbyshire DE6 IDA England
Tel: 01335 347349 Fax: 01335 347303

Rent-a-Hostel

For freedom, flexibility and choice, choose Rent-a-Hostel accommodation for your walking holiday.

The YHA's Rent-a-Hostel scheme is ideal for groups of friends, families and organisations wishing to rent a Youth Hostel.

Freedom! *Renting a Youth Hostel is an exciting way to explore the countryside for people on a budget, giving you and your group the freedom to come and go as you please.*

Flexibility! *Self-catering facilities are available. Alternatively, you may choose to take advantage of Rent-a-Hostel Plus and have meals provided during your stay. Available at some hostels, guests are given the option to unwind while home cooked meals are prepared for them.*

Choice! *With 237 Youth Hostels throughout England and Wales, including 78 on the Rent-a-Hostel sceme, the choice is yours. In great locations, each hostel has its own unique character, from stone cottages to Swis style chalets.*

For your great escape choose Rent-a-Hostel with the YHA.

Rent-a-Hostel is very popular so book early to avoid disappointment. For more information call our Central Bookings Service. Our staff will be happy to help you choose the best to suit your requirements. For details of the Peak District Hostels involved, see page 147.

Contact our Central Bookings Service Now on:
01772 337494

LANDMARK
Publishing Ltd ● ● ● ●

Youth Hosteller's
Walking Guides

(each title £7.99, A5 size)

This series consists of most attractive hand-drawn walking maps of the best routes between and around youth hostels in each area, together with descriptions of these chosen routes and details of the hostel facilities.

Titles in this series also contain a voucher entitling the reader to one year's free membership of the Youth Hostel Association (England & Wales), a saving of £10.00; free accommodation at a YHA hostel (to a maximum of £10.00); or similar.

Available from all good book shops and from:
Landmark Publishing, 12 Compton, Ashbourne, Derbyshire DE6 IDA.
Tel: 01335 347349 Fax: 01335 347303

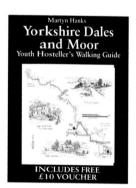

Similar format to the above, covering youth hostels in the Yorkshire Dales and North York Moors. Chiefly covers walks around youth hostels. There is also a 4-hostel upper dales walk and a 3-hostel lower dales walk. **INCLUDES A FREE YHA OVERNIGHT ACCOMMODATION VOUCHER (MAXIMUM £10).** ISBN No: 1-901522-20 2, 208 pages

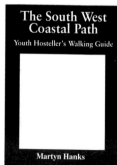

Covers about 40 youth hostels on or close to the coast in Somerset, Devon, Cornwall & Dorset, many set in incomparable locations. **INCLUDES A FREE YHA VOUCHER (DETAILS TO BE ANNOUNCED)** publication date June 1999. ISBN No 1-901522-51 2, 192 pages